This Bursting Sound Within

This Bursting Sound Within

*Selected Works from the COMPAS
Creative Classroom Program*

Edited by
Daniel Gabriel

Cover art by
Shakun Maheshwari

Interior illustrations by
Fiona Avocado

COMPAS
Creative Classroom Program
2017

Publication of this book is generously supported by the Lillian Wright and C. Emil Berglund Foundation, dedicated in memory of C. Emil Berglund.

COMPAS programs are made possible in part by grants provided by the Minnesota State Arts Board, through an appropriation by the Minnesota State Legislature. Additional support has been provided by many generous individuals, corporations, and foundations, which can be found at our website: www.compas.org/partners.

As always, we are grateful for the hundreds of excellent teachers throughout Minnesota who sponsor COMPAS Creative Classroom activities. Without their support and hard work, the writers and artists would not weave their magic, and the student work we celebrate in this book would not spring to life.

Book production: Julie Strand, Huong Nguyen and Emma E-M Seeley, COMPAS staff

Book design: Emma E-M Seeley, COMPAS staff

ISBN 978-0-927663-62-5

Cover art © 2017 by Shakun Maheshwari
Interior illustrations © 2017 by Fiona Avocado
Music, additional words, arrangements © 2017 by Charlie Maguire and Mello-Jamin Music
Text © 2017 COMPAS
All rights reserved. No portion of this book may be reprinted or reproduced without the prior written permission of COMPAS, except for brief passages cited in reviews.

COMPAS
75 Fifth Street West, Suite 304
St. Paul, Minnesota 55102
COMPAS.org

TABLE OF CONTENTS

Introduction   Daniel Gabriel   xi

1: Who I Am   1

Being Myself	Dakota Lueck	2
Where I'm From	Amelia Crone	3
The Things That Make Me Tick	Rylee Steinborn	5
The Roots Within Us	Lay Lay	6
Memory Lane	Mrs. Napierala's Class	8
Gettings A's	Ayub Abdi	9
Braces	Bushra Jama	11
Anxiety Poem	Hailey Dahl	13
I Feel Like a Ghost	Juman Alkhatib	14
Nameless	Ivy Raya	15
Pretty	Sara Lucía Luna Apodaca	16
Happy Man	Abdirahman Warsame	19
The Passing Years	Kensington Tafelmeyer	21
My Footing	Natalia Louise Johnson	22
Who I Am	Jack Dennis Ammann	23
Tongue Waltz	Cristina Furness Rubio	24

2: Speaking Up/Speaking Out   27

The Weight of the World	Henry Hilton	28
Pride	Dahabo Mohamed	29
Bus of Tears	Mauricio Vergara Quiroz	31
Black Hawk	M. M.	33

War in Ethiopia	Matia Solomon	34
Stop Judging	Mahamed Ibrahim & Mustafa Yusuf	35
The Day	Nasrin Awad	37
White Silence	Megan Sumera	38
What the World Needs	Noah Markfort	39
Anchor	Ekhlas Abdullahi & Nafiso Mohamed	41
Of the Six Moro People Who Survived (a sestina)	Beatrix Del Carmen	44
Shoutout to the Losers	Allison Rosenquist	46

3: The World Around Us   49

The Journey	Shea Becker	50
Let's Go Camping	Mr. Crosby's Class	51
I Am a Lake	Adrian Cotter	52
I Am the Woods	Brody Breen	53
Tree	Maverick Wolff	54
Hello Deer	Frannie Eldredge	55
Dear Wolf	Hannah Hagg	56
Sleeping Cat	Gianna Reynolds	57
The Mysterious Black Cat	Tavie Puklich	58
A Climate Change Exchange	Qais Stovall	59
Venezuela	Susana Torrence	61
Caribbean Bracelet	Samantha Fernandez	62
Childhood	Max Opitz	63
Working on a Building	Mr. Terrones' Class	65

4: Finding New Forms   67

Don't Trash Me	Sarah Bagley	68
If My Pen Was a Magic Wand	Signe Elftmann	69
A Day in the Life of Ferox	L. P.	71
Recipe for: Everyone	Karina Hydrie	74
Recipe for: Do You, Be You, Be-you-ti-ful	Lucy Dosch	75
Six-Word Memoirs	Gabrianna Vasquez	76
Being a Princess Is Not So Great	V. P. G.	77
The Scooter	Muajtsim (TJ) Yang	78
Energy: History/Consequences/Solutions	Mrs. Reichgelt's Class	80

5: What Life Throws at Us   89

I Am the One	Hannah Myers	90
Semi-Iceberg	Michaelsan Her	93
Ruined Childhood	Htoo Eh Say	95
I Should Have Stayed in Bed Today	S. C.	97
My Life Lived	Daisy Johnstun	98
It Was Fine	Elliot Tuck	105
Come Abroad the Train of Pain	Annelise Daniels	106
I Wish	Kathy Gao Ia Yang	108
Fear Starts with C	Skyllar Schoening	111
Never	N. E.	114

6: Diving into Adventure   117

One Beautiful Thing	Elizabeth Ekman	118
Almost Average	Aiden Nagorski	122
My Mom's a Spy	Charlotte Mitlyng	124

The Most Amazing Letter!	Lauren Stueber	126
Emily and the Portal to Ralana	Charlotte Carlston	128
The Flood	Atticus Wolford	131
Forgotten Kingdom	Aditya Rewalliwar	133
All Because of a Storm	Sophia Davig	135
William's Cash	Wyatt Cummings	137

7: Wondering — 141

In My Head	Natalie Hughes	142
Stars	Faith Rudnick	143
Mansion	Emma Joswiak-McLaughlin	144
I Prefer	Miya Horel	146
Dear God	Santos Aguirre	147
Pearls of Wisdom	Mrs. Goetzke's Class	148
Common Sense	Eman Abdullahi, Sundus Mohamed & Suado Muqtasid	149
Untitled Assumptions	D. N.	151
Confusion Is an Ocean	Ella Helgeson	152
Highway Corner	Kate Hanf	153
The Playground (from different ages)	Eavan Bobbe	154

Index by Student Writer — 156
Index by School — 159
COMPAS Creative Classroom Teaching Writers — 162
COMPAS Mission and Programs — 163
COMPAS Staff — 165

COMPAS Board of Directors	166
Lillian Wright Awards for Creative Writing	167
Lillian Wright Awards Judge	169
Minnesota Legacy Amendment	170

INTRODUCTION

For decades now, COMPAS has been sending the writers in its Creative Classroom Program out into the schools and communities of Minnesota. What began as a handful of poets in the late sixties, working mostly in Twin Cities urban schools, has expanded into a thriving statewide network of songwriters, storymakers, playwrights, comedians, graphic novelists, spoken word artists and beyond. The forms may change, but at the center of it all remain WORDS, and the ability—nay, the necessity—to communicate.

Who are we? Where did we come from? Where are we going? Why do people hate? fear? love? These are timeless questions—yet how often do we expect our children to voice them, let alone propose answers?

Out of all those classrooms, and all those clever exercises designed to move reluctant writers past barriers, COMPAS writers and artists selected the best for submission to this book. From that group, we have gone further, and selected the best of the best. The range of styles and topics is boggling. We get everything from the complexity and sophistication of Ekhlas Abdullahi and Nafiso Mohamed's "Anchor" to the pure joy of "Let's Go Camping" by the energetic kindergartners of Mr. Crosby's class. We get marvelous fantasy adventures (see virtually the entire section of "Diving into Adventure"), noble tirades against injustice (note especially the "Speaking Up/Speaking Out" section), and bold revelations and questions about the world.

Remember the last time you fled your homeland in fear and had to resettle in a new country where people spoke an unknown tongue? Me neither. But some of these students do, and the insights they provide are crucial. Just check "The Roots Within Us" by Lay Lay and see if your perspective isn't enlarged. Ivy Raya considers the impact of adoption in "Nameless": "My name is who I am, but it has been changed throughout time. Does that mean that I have changed as well?" Hailey Dahl exposes feelings that many of us have in "Anxiety Poem":

"It's like a little creature
Sitting on your shoulder
Telling you you're not worth anyone's time
Or that everything you're doing is wrong
You push people away before they get the chance to abandon you."

Powerful stuff, that.

Equally powerful to me are those pieces that offer an almost prescient sense of time passing, never to be regained. My favorite in this vein is Eavan Bobbe's poem "The Playground."

Replete with imagery and wistfulness, it serves as an epitaph to childhood.

Throughout these pieces, there is a sense that the young writers are often responding to an internal imperative to make their voices heard. It's that entire concept of "this is something that I can't keep from saying" that brought me the title of the book. Cristina Furness Rubio concludes her epic linguistic paeon to the Catalan language ("Tongue Waltz") with the words:

"I am from this bursting sound within."

That's what fifth grader Henry Hilton had in mind, when he wrote:

"A whole page flowing out
Of my brain and onto the page.
A sea of thoughts expressed.
The weight of the world
On a piece of paper."

Let the sea of thoughts heave and foam…rejoice that the bursting sound comes forth!

—Daniel Gabriel, editor

Section 1:
Who I Am

COMPAS

Being Myself

I express my true inside.
I do what I say, not what other people may.
I am myself, no matter if I'm far away,
No matter if it's night or day.
I'll be myself and with that,
I could do anything.
I could soar as far as an eagle,
I could move as swiftly as a hare.
I could roar as loud as a lion,
I could be as strong as a bear.
I would shine so bright,
I would stand so tall.
I am myself.
And with that,
I'll never fall.
Ages pass by, and I'm a beacon of right!
If I'm myself,
Then I will stay myself.
Others may say differently,
But only they don't see the light.
Many are blinded, just looking at…
Me.
The one…
And the only.
Because I express my true inside.

Dakota Lueck, Grade 5
Hillcrest Community School, Bloomington
Teaching Artist, Frank Sentwali

Where I'm From

I come from memories
Almost all saved in my mother's many scrapbooks
I am from failed pets
From cats to gerbils to grasshoppers
I am from my sister's tears and the flush of the toilet

I am from the pictures on my wall
I am from pine trees standing tall
All winter
I am from my grandma's garden
And the barking of her dog
At any person who chooses to pass by

I am from my grandfather
I am from that snowy day
When my sister and I skipped home to one less grandparent

I am from my abuelita
Who at 14 had to come to the land of the free
And make a life for herself
I am from stories and little Ecuadorian candies
I am from old cookie recipes and off-tune Christmas songs

I am from Windom Elementary
With its school carnivals and read-a-thons
Where crushes were based off of who ran the fastest
Or who did the best math
Not personalities
Or even looks

I am from every day of my life
From cherished to forgotten memories
I am from my friends
My family
My past
My life
I come from memories

Amelia Crone, Grade 7
Anwatin Middle School, Minneapolis
Teaching Artist, Frank Sentwali

The Things That Make Me Tick

I am from the pull of the rod and the reel,
The force in my arms,
The confidence I get from the size of the fish.

I am from the kick of the gun against my shoulder,
The excitement of sighting the deer,
The loudness in your ear.

I am from the smell of freshly cut wood,
The buzzing of the saw,
The vibrations in my hand
That continue even after I'm done.

Rylee Steinborn, Grade 6
LeSueur-Henderson Middle School, Le Sueur
Teaching Artist, SEE MORE PERSPECTIVE

The Roots Within Us

The color I'm in, the music I bring, the dance I represent,
is the culture!
No! Wait! It's the root within me.
I was 7 years old,
was just learning to read Karen.
Karen; do you guys know Karen?
Most people don't:
When I say "oh I'm Karen"
They correct me,
"Korean?"
No! I'm not Korean.
I . Am. Karen.
The people of the mountains: who are still on the run seeking
freedom and democracy.
BUT—constantly being dehumanized, denied, and
differentiated by the very people trusted:
GENOCIDE took over.
You see the Karens were the ones who lived in mountains,
and drank from the flowing waterfall,
And it was considered "Different."
This left the cleaners to scrub us off; saying we don't fit the
"Burmese Ideal."
Like a fly in the house we're chased and killed: it was as if
Hitler owned the house.
Just like that, I wondered if freedom and democracy are just a
fantasy.
On the other hand, my Karens who escaped this inhumane
genocide…
I wonder if they are still aware
or if they have just abandoned the thought.
Because just like me they came young,
in a new world, like a butterfly out of its cocoon:

Trying to live and represent Karen BUT—
"You should only speak English here."
"Can you talk where we can understand?"
The society we thought welcomed us, also tried to "clean" us.
Slowly like that…a ROOT within us got pulled out.
As we let this continue, the songs the tradition and music of Karen
disappear into a fathomless world, floating around trying to be heard and remembered again!
"Wuh luh ghay."
"No, good morning."
Did I hear a voice speak?
BAM! Another root pulled.
As I struggle to keep my root,
there are many Karen who are already rootless!
And just to be even more rootless!
We look upon pop culture, new technology, and the influences on these wandering souls;
pull them further and further and further away from Remembering! Recognizing!
The fights that our people have endured every day.
We are rare tigers—brave yet powerless.
Will we as youth let others make us become assimilationists?
Because the only way we can avoid this is by calling back the songs, dance and music of our heritage;
when that happens
our roots will sink back—and regrow to bloom into a beautiful flower on the very mountain our roots started.

Lay Lay, Grade 8
Humboldt Senior High School, Saint Paul
Teaching Artist, Frank Sentwali

 Memory Lane

Before we say goodbye, let's go down memory lane
All the way from Kindergarten to Fifth Grade
Step by step—year by year
All the time, and days that we've been here!

In Kindergarten we made crafts
Of the Solar System and the animal masks
"Book Buddies" read to us
A long recess for fun stuff

Pictures of our families
Along with the houses and the trees
In Second Grade we performed in plays
And made pots for Mothers Day

Endangered species on display
In dioramas in Third Grade
We laid on the floor and we were traced
And put our "organs" in their place

We worked in groups for the exhibition
And talked of technologies' ambition
The "Memoir Tea Party" was so fun
The mints melted on our tongues

It all started on the first day
Then we were on our way
It all started on the first day
Then we were on our way

Mrs. Napierala's Class, Grade 5
Highland Park Elementary School, Saint Paul
Teaching Artist, Charlie Maguire

Getting A's

Getting A's is a wonderful thing.
It makes me so happy I wanna sing.
My blood goes in a flow.
While I get 5 straight A's in a row.
People say I'm as smart as a calculator, but I study right now or later.
Getting A's doesn't only mean you're smart it means you're great.
All those tests for me await.
When I get A's it feels like the test gives me a high-five.
I wonder what I will do in my life.
Teacher teaches those tremendous students.
While other students get apartments.
I write essays on pages, while other students are in cages.
I feel happy when my teacher says I'm outrageous.
The teacher says it's time to take the test.
I know that I'll do my best.
When I took the test it felt like hours.
I thought that if I passed I'd get flowers.
My principal said don't listen to the haters and the dominators.
I got my pencil and my calculator.
The first question felt hard.
After that the test got easy.
When the windows were up, I felt breezy.
My blood felt like it ran a race.
My brain works like it has beat fear.
When I got my test back I had an A+.
I started going down in tears.
I felt tall and big as a tree and a big fierce lion.
I felt joy taking over while I gave my mom a hug.

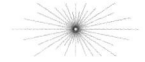

That whole day I felt as if I had powers.
Getting A's means that I'm smart and awesome.
Getting A's made me happy.

Ayub Abdi, Grade 9
Rochester STEM Academy, Rochester
Teaching Artist, Frank Sentwali

Braces

Just being 8
Doesn't mean you have to wait
It's my time to be a star sparkle shine
Soon to be looking fine
Sitting on the chair
When putting on, you can feel the pain
It's like biting into your own tongue instead of a candy cane
OUCH!
Then the best part, choosing the color
Y'all know blues the best
Minnesota's #1 and also mine
Doctors be setting the rules
But I ignore them, just call me cool
All they say is no candy, no caramel, no pop
But I just hear yes candy, yes caramel, yes pop
I come home wanting to eat
But I can't because of the brackets
I take one bite
Then it feels like my mouth is having a fight
I got them off two years later and
Got them back on two years more
The first time was simply to fix my overbite
This time was easy, better than the first
I see my teeth getting better and better
It's time and only the last time
The wires, the colors, the brackets
Seeing them on for the last time in my mouth
It's like the braces were saying, goodbye,
And sobbing a waterfall
They have all the tools by my side
Taking the wires off is like bumping into a cactus

Then scraping the glue is a jungle of toughness
But it's okay, I'm in a land called happiness
Yeah! They're off
But it feels so slimy like a jellyfish's jelly
I look at them and say, "are these my teeth?"
I keep staring and staring
And finally find my smile
I might have been called a brace face
But now look, I have a retainer case

Bushra Jama, Grade 9
Rochester STEM Academy, Rochester
Teaching Artist, Frank Sentwali

Anxiety Poem

Racing heart
Restless mind
Sweaty palms
Sleepless nights

I get anxiety but nobody other than me seems to notice
Nobody seems to notice when I'm deep in thought
Everyone thinks that anxiety is just some mind thing
Anxiety is NOT something you make up!

It's real
The endless doubt
The nonstop thinking

It's all real!

It's like there's a little creature
Sitting on your shoulder
Telling you you're not worth anyone's time
Or that everything you're doing is wrong

You push people away before they get the chance to abandon you first

Anxiety is not just all mental
"Torture" basically

Anxiety comes with chest pain
Along with hyperventilating and vomiting
It also comes with feelings of being lonely
Even if your friends are all around

Hailey Dahl, Grade 9
Roseau Secondary School, Roseau
Teaching Artist, Frank Sentwali

I Feel Like a Ghost

I feel like a ghost
where nobody can see
me like I don't exist or a shadow
hiding behind a brave soul
who likes to express their
self to the world. If a
person cared about my feelings
I would be a brave soul
with a big shadow full
of scared hidden ghosts.

Juman Alkhatib, Grade 4
Creek Valley Elementary, Edina
Teaching Artist, Becca Barniskis

Nameless

"Chun Lee!" my mother calls softly. "Chun Lee, wake up!" I awake slowly, my eyes still adjusting to the light. I see my mother standing above me. She says, "It's time to go home."

I feel myself getting lifted up out of the crib, taken to a place I've never been before, somehow knowing that I'm supposed to be there. Slowly letting drowsiness take over knowing I'm safe.

The days pass and suddenly I'm called by a new name, Ivalee Raya. The days turning to months turning to years and I'm called yet another name, short enough for people to pronounce correctly, and unique enough to get excited when I meet someone with the same name.

Used over and over again until the name is worn thin; used too many times that it has lost its meaning. My name is who I am, but it has been changed throughout time. Does that mean that I have changed as well?

Ivy Raya, Grade 6
St. Paul Academy, Saint Paul
Teaching Artist, May Lee-Yang

Pretty

Pretty I am
    Pretty I'll be
Pretty we'll always be but
                      Beautiful we'll always keep

Pretty she is
    Handsome he'll be

But this world wants to define who we want to be

Pretty I am
    Pretty I'll be

    But the roots within will never define the beautiful
Flower that will bloom from deep in

Pretty she is
    Handsome he'll be

But society will always remind us that having curves is not that good of a thang

Pretty I am
    Pretty I'll be
But this world has to stop telling me what to be

           I'll never be good
           I'll never be high
         Nor will I ever be low

    The way you define me

Won't matter to me
You can call me this
You can call me that

    But your words will always be like poison
And thank god I have a mask

Just like a flower I will rise way
    Beyond the dirty words that you lie

 Just like you we all seek attention

But deep within we all look for
    Perfection

But we think we have to give people perfection

But what we don't see are

                                             The
                                              Words
                                                     That
                                                          Lie

                                    Behind

The
   Words
      That
         Hide
            Is

What we want to be like

We all want to be Kim we want to
        Be Kiley
                But
                        That's too
                                Much money

Am I still pretty enough for this society?

        Pretty I am
                Pretty I'll be
But I know that deep within
I'll always be me and that's all my mama needs

Sara Lucía Luna Apodaca, Grade 7
Richfield Middle School, Richfield
Teaching Artist, Frank Sentwali

Happy Man

I am a happy man
'Cause I'm trying to do the best I can
I know that I am not the richest
Nor am I the smartest
But you know what I am, a happy man

Wherever I went I stuck out like a thorn in a pail of daisies
So I tried to put myself in other people's shoes
It didn't work out for me and man was it boring
so I went back to being a thorn
Because I form from the stem of the most beautiful flower the rose
I am a happy man
In a world where people reject what is different
I accept it with all my heart
Different sticks out like the A in stem
I don't care what trial and tribulation awaits me in the future
Because I know Allah will not burden a soul beyond that which it can bear
Thanks to god I am a happy man

People working for hours just to get a lot of money
Thinking that money can buy you happiness
Not knowing that happiness is a quality of the soul
And can't be found in material things like money
Because happiness is found when 99% of the things you do and say are for others
Knowing this, I am a happy man

God has blessed me with many things that I didn't ask for
Allah has given his eye and some have eyes but they can't see
He gave me ears and some have ears but they can't hear
He gave me a mouth and others have mouths but they can't speak
And because of this blessing I am happy

I have a roof over my head
I have food to eat
I have clothes to wear
I have an education
This is why I'm a happy man

Abdirahman Warsame, Grade 9
Rochester STEM Academy, Rochester
Teaching Artist, Frank Sentwali

The Passing Years

I am from a big tan house with a garage that has a back room.
I am from the grill where dad makes chicken wings to have with Spanish rice.
I am from the tractor that took five fingers from my uncle, the chair that broke my brother's collar bone.
I am from the trip to Wyoming, watching a bear cub and its mother.
I am from the school that taught me to read and write.
I am from the shade of the pine trees, soft green moss crawling up their trunks.
I am from a kitchen were mom makes chocolate chip cookies.
I am from a Christmas long ago with family sitting next to me, telling stories by the fire.
I am from the yard where I had many fun years playing with my dog Patch, I'm from the church where Sunday school is always fun.

Kensington Tafelmeyer, Grade 4
Kittson Central Elementary, Hallock
Teaching Artist, Marie Olofsdotter

My Footing

I am from the soul-full strong wildlife
I am from the soothing sound
I am from the bird song
And river sound
I am from the potassium and calcium
I am from a family who I love
Driving and fixing cars
And speaking Spanish
I am from the strong pluck of the string
And the low note of the woodwind
I am from outside where the sound-full
Muddy river flows
Where the fast current
Moves swiftly with the trees
In the water with the bobbers
Bringing the shiny gray fish to the top
I am from the light green
Levels of the tall tree
I am from the black dark starlit night
With the owls hooting and the crickets
Playing their humming midnight song
I am from the animals howling like
Wolves to the moon
I am from a small sweet town
I am from school
I am from music
And my family's sweet love

Natalia Louise Johnson, Grade 7
Roseau Secondary School, Roseau
Teaching Artist, Rachel Moritz

Who I Am

I am from
Horseback in the civil war, delivering messages that would otherwise be untold;
I travel from war to war in the armed forces
now hoping I don't get shot like the dead guy lying next to me for he will rot.
I have descended from good ol' country living, where there is hot food on the stove.
The life all them city slickers will never know.

I am from
Hard work in the fields carrying potatoes on your back
at a young age, helping support a family where I want to stay.
I am shipped when the twins came to the world.
Where you work for the neighbors just to stay alive,
You'll do anything if the situation is live or die.

I am from
A warrior at heart, battling multiple sclerosis from day to day
hoping and praying that he'll stay on earth
and we will take it day by day.
There are no borders where I'm from,
coming from foreign countries.

Jack Dennis Ammann, Grade 7
LeSueur Henderson Middle School, Le Sueur
Teaching Artist, SEE MORE PERSPECTIVE

Tongue Waltz

I am from Catala.
Different, rolling
tongue.
Gorgeous, colorful
& bright words
overfilling my
mind.
I share a piece
of it with you.

"aquest llenguatge,
les meves paraules genials
que ningú enten."

"What is that?"
You ask,
"a version of Spanish?
Something you made up?"

"No,
Catala," I tell you.

"Can you repeat that?"

"CA-TA-LA"

It's different, I know.

A mouse in the
midst of hungry
cats

alone, endangered
yet... I am overflowing
with this need to scream
it out loud,
"aquest llenguatge,
les meves paraules genials
que ningú enten."

You ask me to say
something more in this new language,
like I knew you would.

As if it wouldn't be real
if no words came with it.
I say something anyway
just to be nice,
but also to impress you.

"aquest llenguatge,
les meves paraules genials
que ningú enten."

My language,
special and flowing.

A secret
that I am dying
to share.

You may think it's weird
Unusual
Japanese?

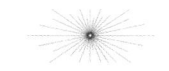

It seems so complex,
and trust me, it is
but I love it just the same.

My language, it's
very meaningful
to me.

It's imaginative
a lone sunflower
relishing the sun
on a warm
summer's day.

I can visualize
a future for myself
and this language
is a part of it.

A secret
that I am
dying to
share.

I am from this bursting sound within.

Cristina Furness Rubio, Grade 7
Richfield Middle School, Richfield
Teaching Artist, SEE MORE PERSPECTIVE

Section 2:
Speaking Up/Speaking Out

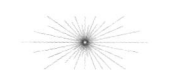

The Weight of the World

The low light
Of the outdoors shrinking like a
Candle about to die. I am more
Alert. Every sound a thunderstorm
To my ears, my hand shakes
Gingerly as I put the dull pencil
To paper scratching out words.
And then a sentence then
A whole page flowing out
Of my brain and onto the page.
A sea of thoughts expressed.
The weight of the world
On a piece of paper.

Henry Hilton, Grade 5
Saint Paul Academy, Saint Paul
Teaching Artist, Julia Klatt Singer

Pride

"She's a part of that religion that condones violence."
When I walk down the streets of the country I call home that is all I hear.
Does my existence cause you some sort of harm?
You stare, point, and call me nothing but a terrorist.
You try to shame me because I choose to follow a religion that I know as peace.

I walk down the streets of the country I am a citizen of with nothing but pride.
But why is it that when I walk those streets I hear nothing but hate?
All you say is, "Don't worry guys Trump will kick her out soon."
Do you not realize your Trump remarks do not scare me one bit?
But why do you want me gone so bad?
What did I do to you?

Is it my fault you associate me with bin Laden?
Is it my fault that when you see me you think ISIS?
I give you the benefit of doubt.
I smile when I see you walk down the streets.
I don't associate you with Hitler.
I don't think you're a part of the KKK.
But why is it that you can't give me the benefit of the doubt that I give you?

All I hear are the lectures of why would I ever want to follow a religion of hate?
But in your eyes it's no lecture, you just frame it like you want the best for me.

But did it not occur to you that your opinion isn't a factor
when I decide the religion I want to practice?
Your curiosity on why I wear a black scarf on a hot summer
day does not make me question the religion that I call peace.

I walk down the streets of the country I was born in with
nothing but pride.
But all I hear are my fellow citizens trying to tear me down.
You telling me to go back to my "pretty disgusting" country
sounds foolish on your part.
This is my country just as much as it is yours.

So please don't bother me when I walk down the streets of
the country I will soon be able to vote in with nothing but my
pride.
So please don't give me an unasked-for lecture when I walk
down the streets of the country that is my joy with nothing
but my pride.

Dahabo Mohamed, Grade 7
Richfield Middle School, Richfield
Teaching Artist, Frank Sentwali

Bus of Tears

The wheels on the bus
They go back to poverty and pain
But they still don't fuss
Yet they think they're insane

The wheels on the bus
Go back to home
But they don't even cuss
Although they have no home

The wheels on the bus
Go back to drugs and corruption
Yet they don't feel their agony
Living in a place of abduction
The wheels on the bus
Yeah they feel no pity
They say friends come and go
But family is forever

Yet they split families
They are unique and work hard
Yet they are hated and exploited
For not knowing English

Still for them there is a sea of hatred
America the free country
What happened to that
Where is the freedom when you're afraid to leave the house

Deported for looking for a better life
Integrity and independence are inspiring

But where is it when they blindly follow
Even if what they follow is wrong
The wheels on the bus
The wheels on the bus
The wheels on the bus
Leave a trail of tears

Mauricio Vergara Quiroz, Grade 7
Richfield Middle School, Richfield
Teaching Artist, Desdamona

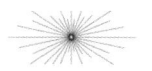

Black Hawk

Past: Black Hawk was a capable and fierce war chief. He led the Sauk tribes in assisting the British in the War of 1812. Then he fought to save his people's land from the settlers. However, he eventually was captured and his people lost their land.

Present: Black Hawk is released and still fighting for his homeland and Natives' equal rights. Black Hawk is definitely against the idea of building a pipeline in Dakota.

Future: Black Hawk has formed lots of groups not based on tribe, but based on confidence and eagerness. He and his people have got ¼ of the United States or their homeland back. They are continually approaching on invading more main states that were, and still are, important to them.

Black Hawk has died, but his people didn't give up. They are still working and fighting to get ½ of their land.

Monologue: I am Black Hawk who thinks the idea of building a pipeline in Dakota is pathetic and useless to me and all Native Americans who live in North Dakota and around the world. What is the point of not building a pipeline in white neighborhoods and building it in an indigenous land? Hmmm… I'm thinking "racism." The pipeline should not be built in North Dakota or anywhere else where it affects…

M. M., Grade 10
Roosevelt High School, Minneapolis
Teaching Artist, Marcie Rendon

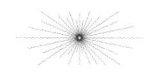

War in Ethiopia

Ethiopia despite where I may roam,
This will always be my home.
The place of my youth
Like a tree, I plant my roots.
A land of rich coffee.
A place where I am free,
Where we eat our biscuits,
And drink our morning tea,
But ever since I've left, you have begun to tumble.
The war is detrimental to your health, making you crumble.
Tribes of one nation seek to gain power.
One tribe rises, leaving the others sour.
We continue to fight, killing our brothers,
Leaving us to forget our beautiful mothers,
But how much is it worth? The money and fame,
Enough to oppress a nation, leaving the innocent to blame.
Men drop, as their blood drips,
While poor hungry children have no water to sip.
And, as a child with hope, I pray every night
That my beautiful nation will find the light,
Despite the fact, there might be no end in sight.

Matia Solomon, Grade 8
North View Middle School, Brooklyn Park
Teaching Artist, Tou SaiKo Lee

Stop Judging

Just stop it...
That is not us, that is not who we are
Please give us a chance
Stop being sentimentally judgmental toward us for others' mistakes.
Like the bombing of 9/11 and ISIS's terrorism
Instead wait...
Look at our perspectives
You've spent so much time differentiating between us
That you have forgotten our similarities and what we share
Try to think that we are both humans and both have feelings
Try to remember that we both value our religion, culture and dignity
Just try to imagine the pain we went through
It really hurts when you say that i am the aggressor
Or have the nerve to look upon me as an oppressor
But really that i am being oppressed
Being called a terrorist when i really am not
My eyes dry from crying so long
Do you even try to understand us?
Who are the people who are bombed in Syria and Iraq
They are MUSLIMS
There are those who use my name to do wrong
But if i do not approve why am i to be blamed
In every religion there are those who do wrong
Thinking they have permission to do so
Who are you to judge us
It really hurts when i am accused of something that i'm not
So again who are you to judge us?
My religion is Islam
And the meaning of Islam is peace and the Qur'an is its proof

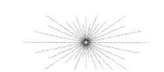

That revealed over 1,400 years ago
Who gave you the power to judge other people
When you don't even judge yourself
You are not god so think twice before you judge others
There are many people who live in this world
Many of them thinking that Islam is all about terrorism
There have been attacks on the US, yes
But, America is not the only place in violent stress
When a person uses a Muslim name to attack even though they are not
The news jumps straight to Islamic terrorism
i would think before i act and clear my ignorance if i were you
For the last time who are you to judge us
Who made this rule to use others as a shield
For the pain you couldn't gasp
Who are you to think that we are somehow worse than you
i am sorry if this sounds unusual but i am merely being realistic
But the way of Islam is to treat those who treat you bitter... better.

Mahamed Ibrahim and Mustafa Yusuf, Grade 11
Rochester STEM Academy, Rochester
Teaching Artist, Frank Sentwali

The Day

Today is the day of change,
The day that changed our history.
The day which shocked many ears,
And fooled many eyes.
Today is the day which makes all of us awake,
And thirsty of more politics.
Today is the day of the unknown outcome,
The day which we don't know where we go from here,
And what the future will hold for us.
Today is the day that worries our parents.
With a lot of struggle, sadness, smiles and laughter,
Today is the day that silenced our faces.
I hope, today is the day that we put all of our differences aside,
And work together as a nation,
For the best of our success.
Today should be the day of our country,
The day which we celebrate together!

Nasrin Awad, Grade 11
Rochester STEM Academy, Rochester
Teaching Artist, Frank Sentwali

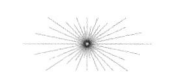

White Silence

White silence is white consent.
By staying silent about police brutality, we are, in a way,
accepting, and promoting, the murders of innocent people.
Only, in some way, in some people's eyes, these are not
people.
Just because they have a different pigmented skin.
It is repulsive.
And this goes beyond the Black Lives Matter protest.
Worldwide, people of color are taken advantage of.
As I speak, Natives are protesting to stop the destruction of
their land and history.
Police and the army have been sent there to oversee and stop
them, if needed.
The government and police are supposed to protect us.
Yet people of color are continually killed and disrespected.
Innocent people.
White silence is white consent.

Megan Sumera, Grade 10
Roosevelt High School, Minneapolis
Teaching Artist, Marcie Rendon

What the World Needs

What the world needs now is not a frown
It does not need anger or a bully
For goodness sake we need kindness and happiness
Just give a smile like an emoji
What the world needs now is not a celebrity
A rock star is out of the picture
It does not need to know the next Charlie Puth or Donald Trump
But a super hero and their power is
Helping
Helping people
We all need cookies to help our hunger of a lion
We need Mrs. Rohl all over to help the brains in life
What the world needs now is not
A dictator or an evil king not a
Hitler or Stalin not even an evil prime minister
The world
Us
We
We need a leader a super hero
As powerful as Batman but their only
Power is helping
The person will provide food and learning
U
Me
USA
China
All
For all

That is what the world needs
Not from anyone
From us

Noah Markfort, Grade 5
Bailey Elementary School, Woodbury
Teaching Artist, Frank Sentwali

Anchor

Ekhlas and Nafiso: 11 years old, alone and isolated, but they claim to be her friends.
Nafiso: Not fitting in, different, not interested in those daily trends.
Her personality so cunningly sweet, kind, and caring.
That smile, so warming and daring,
But she was the one who got picked.

Ekhlas and Nafiso: Picked, the one who got picked on, the one who was talked about.
Ekhlas: The one who wanted the hole in her heart to go away, but instead it keeps coming back.
Staying focused, ignoring all the bickering, staying on track,
Screaming! Leave me alone, asking God for the facts.
But instead she waits for her grief to go away.

Ekhlas and Nafiso: 12 years old, running home tears coming down her face.
Nafiso: Wondering, why is this happening to me?
Afraid to tell her parents, not wanting them to worry.
Those tears in her eyes, she can't see anything, all blurry.

Ekhlas: She pushed her emotions away,
Her eyes lifeless and dull,
It seemed as if she was absorbing the words,
Letting them sink into her body.

Ekhlas and Nafiso: 13 years old, she got them curves, trying to hide them with big clothes, insecure.
Nafiso: Ashamed. Ashamed of how she looked, ashamed of the way she dressed,

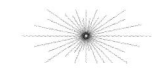

Ashamed of the way god created her, but instead she throws it all away.
Those dark thoughts creeping up on her as she stares at the knife,
Those dark feelings urging her to end her sad cold life.
She tries to reach for the light,
But who will guide her?

Ekhlas: Months later her light finally came, bright as the sun yet subtle as the moon.
A bystander watching as she suffered,
Noticed the scars on her arms.
As if she was adorning her body with their insults
trying to bleed out the pain,
Her anger only directed towards herself.

But she was scared, scared of the fact that she will be the one who will get picked.
Or she will face suicide, she will face Darkness
Because Darkness is a part of us.

Nafiso: Alone she walked down the halls, looking over her shoulder, hearing her name
Grabbing her bag, feeling tamed she wondered why do I have this fame?
Steps, so close to her house.
The first thing she does is grab a knife.
Those Darkness thoughts in her head again…
Voices saying you're better off dead. She is ready to go; she is ready to leave.
A young woman ending her life at fourteen.

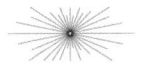

Ekhlas: Fourteen years old, her plan was to face death and get over society.
She lost her dignity, her faith in believing she has a chance...
Off the cliff she goes, at the tip of the roof about to say goodbye,
But the bystander comes in time, saves her life and becomes her sunshine. Her anchor saving her from that cold wretched death,
Promising never to lose to society ever again.

Nafiso: Let this be a lesson to those who bully and to those who watch,
Watching them end their lives like a game of hopscotch.
Time is ticking, stop looking at your wristwatch.
Death does not fear.
Stand next to your friend and wipe away their tears.

Ekhlas Abdullahi and Nafiso Mohamed, Grade 9
Rochester STEM Academy, Rochester
Teaching Artist, Frank Sentwali

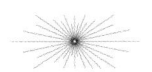

Of the Six Moro People Who Survived (a sestina)

(a response to a photo of American soldiers posed with the dead bodies of one thousand Filipino Muslims, known as Moros, after the Moro Crater Massacre of 1906)

of trauma; of fear; of war forgotten
in between the lines of generation; I speak
to you of rebellion; trampled and buried
beneath five feet of brown body
as they stood posed; hungry; like glory hounds
we watch our Moro blood redden Sulu waters

our cries slip into rising tides; water
laughing over shallow chants as we attempt to forget
the feeling of trampling hounds
of silent battles; cutout mouths that continue to speak
they claim to save us while leaving our bodies
to be lifeless props; broken and battered and never buried

our history snapped into pieces and buried
across seven thousand islands; our stories watered
down and used to clean the scars off their bodies
this was our land first and we won't forget
that it was our culture before they ever spoke
of law; of lesson; of a greatness they crave to hound

in Jolo we stood united; eyes fierce into seas of war hounds
meet barrels of shiny guns; bare feet buried
in crater's edge; blades of Kris line up and speak
sharply of resistance; we epitomize untamed water
as we flood foreign armies; we'd rather be dead than forgotten
they will remember our eyes as we meld into one body

strong for three suns and three stars, our bodies
still chopped into pieces; hunted and fed to the hounds
heartlessly; cut up mouths cry 'we won't be forgotten'

as our limbs pile; a massacre soon buried
beneath the silent verses of scapegoat; melts into water
to nourish palm trees; leaves now singing rebellion for our
lips that cannot speak
and we are the six who remain; who can no longer speak
of resilience without speaking through throats of blood; red
covered bodies
cloud our vision so we wash our eyes in Sulu water
and stare into what is left of Bud Dajo; remember the hounds
who kicked dust over corpses; burying
truth with disassembled flesh and left to be forgotten
our skinny six bodies; heavy with forget
we speak of this suffering so as not to bury
our stories into our waters and be drunk by the hounds

Beatrix Del Carmen, Grade 11
Perpich Center for Arts Education, Golden Valley
Teaching Artist, Kyle Tran Myhre (Guante)

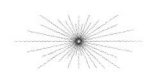

Shoutout to the Losers

Shoutout to the losers
The fallers, the failers
The weak links and the derailers
The movers and the shakers
The world changers
The speakers who sound like screamers
The dancers who move like believers
Those of us who climb and fall and climb and fall
Who run for the sake of running
Who survive for the sake of loving
Those of us who would rather sing like a broken tea kettle
with a purpose
Than spend our lives silent and powerless
Dear loser,
Don't let them bring you down
Please know that those who cause pain will cause pain
regardless of how hard you try to change
So you might as well live a little
Those other people being strong does not make you any less
powerful
Your friends being beautiful does not make you ugly

Dear loser,
Know that dad jokes
Are awesome
And if doing the sprinkler
And the Hokey Pokey make you feel alive
Then dance
If pastel scrunchies and turtlenecks make you feel freaking
fergalicious
Then own it

If climbing is your poetry in motion
Than climb
Your mountain is waiting
Stumbling over loose pebbles and tripping on broken fears
You can fall a thousand times
Before realizing that reaching the top looks a lot like failing with pride
If you feel for one second that you aren't worth it
Think of every person that loves you and why
Know that self-love is not an act of arrogance
Self-hatred is not an act of philanthropy
You are cherished
Your body is a beautiful gift
No matter what it is or isn't
Know that there are some demons that cannot be silenced
Please believe me when I say you won't have to face them alone
Even if you fall
Even if you stumble on broken footsteps
Even if each breath proves how hard you are trying
Each breath is proof at how hard I am trying
To make you try to breathe
In reality you can let the world change you
Or you can let yourself change the world

We see what we are looking to find
If you are looking for something to hate you will see it in everyone
Your bitter breath will slowly become you
But if you look for something to love you will find yourself enamored with the universe that cared for you enough to bring you into itself
That trying to change people without trying to understand

them will only cause pain
That we all have the right to be fluid in our convictions
We can bloom in sweeping valleys
We just have to plant the seeds
So go ahead
Start running
Cut your hair off
Tell that person you love why you love them
Tell that person you hate why you know there is good in them
Travel to Indonesia
Learn French
Bake a cake
Use your voice
Take your life by the reins
'Cause you can float with the tide or you can surf
And even if you fail at everything you enter
Know that some loser is watching on the sidelines wishing they had your bravery to try
That by failing with grace and complexity you are showing them that they have the power
All they have to do is start

Allison Rosenquist, Grade 8
Oak Hill Montessori, Shoreview
Teaching Artist, Desdamona

Section 3:
The World Around Us

The Journey

Bring me on a journey of peace,
where the saddest times come alive
and then slowly fade away,
where everything is calm
and the only thing you can hear
are the good memories and the best times,
where you don't have to suffer
if you choose not to,
where anything is possible
with peace.

Shea Becker, Grade 4
Meadowbrook Elementary, Golden Valley
Teaching Artist, Marie Olofsdotter

Let's Go Camping!

Let's go camping you and me
We'll leave town for the lakes and trees
We'll live in a tent, we'll sleep on the ground
Let's go camping, we got it down!

Camping means a fire at night
Making s'mores they taste alright
It's getting dark, and I can't see
It's the sleeping bag for me

Let's go camping, we'll fish all day
Let's go for a hike, that's what I say
Let's have hot dogs after the hike
With lots of ketchup and mustard, that's what I like

Down to the lake to take a dip
Then out of the water to take a sip
The raccoons with their burglar masks
Robbed our food and ate it fast

We'll have to walk or get a canoe
Back to the market to get more food
One hundred dollars and ten cents
For more food to bring back to the tent!

Mr. Crosby's Class, Kindergarten
St. Anthony Park Elementary School, Saint Paul
Teaching Artist, Charlie Maguire

I Am a Lake

I am a lake swishing and shushing
I am a tadpole getting put in a jar
I am a rock rolling by the current
I am moss growing on a rock
I am a salmon swimming against the current
I am a stick floating on the water
I am a waterbug teasing the fish
I am a lily hanging on with all my might
I am a snake gliding through the water
I am a current pulling things back
I am a frog sticking out my tongue to get food
I am a waterfall splashing into a stream

Adrian Cotter, Grade 3
Mendota Elementary, Mendota Heights
Teaching Artist, Susan Marie Swanson

I Am the Woods

I am the ice holding
the stream's ripples,
I am the stream
watering the trees,
I am the trees giving
home to a squirrel,
I am a squirrel
taking the leaves
for my bed, I am
the leaves falling
on the woods, I am
the woods.

Brody Breen, Grade 2
Oak Ridge Elementary School, Eagan
Teaching Artist, Susan Marie Swanson

Tree

You smell like a musty attic, armor flaking off and spiraling down as I ascend.
Your canopy protects your friends from the harsh surroundings.
Strong arms standing firm in the wind.
You watched as I fell and then screamed, wishing you could do something.
But I wasn't mad.
I came back.
And every year you come back.

Maverick Wolff, Grade 6
Saint Paul Academy, Saint Paul
Teaching Artist, May Lee-Yang

Hello Deer

Hello Deer,
with your antlers.
You scram away when
someone sees you.
I always find you
in the woods
eating on some grass,
leaping over a bush,
jumping over a tree stump,
hiding under a pile of sticks.
Why are you always alone?
You're similar to a fox.
You're mostly golden when I see you.
You're chewing on some bark.
You are very silent,
Why are you so silent?
You are not scared of night.
You don't give anyone a fright.
You are very peaceful,
going with the flow.

Frannie Eldredge, Grade 2
Mendota Elementary School, Mendota Heights
Teaching Artist, Susan Marie Swanson

Dear Wolf

Dear Wolf,
The moon is up.
Come and howl to the moon.
Your howling is so fantastic.
After, go to the forest,
The one with the most trees.
You'll find food to eat
That's your favorite.
Come closer, by the rock,
By the cave
And I will be there
To ask questions about you.

Your friend,
Hannah

Hannah Hagg, Grade 2
Gleason Lake Elementary School, Plymouth
Teaching Artist, Julia Klatt Singer

Sleeping Cat

Here is my cat sleeping
so silently in
her cat tower,
so still.
She's hearing calmness
like a person sleeping
in the night hearing
calmness too. My cat
is looking at the
stars so bright
they light up
in her eyes,
like the stars
are looking right back
at my cat
winking, my cat
thinking how
delightful the
wink was.

Gianna Reynolds, Grade 4
Mendota Elementary School, Mendota Heights
Teaching Artist, Susan Marie Swanson

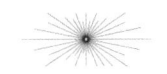

The Mysterious Black Cat

There was an abandoned barn. The barn was a brownish, reddish color. The brown door was creaky when I opened it. I walked inside. The floor was brown wood. The walls were also brown wood. There was a brown bookshelf with lots of books. I took a brown leather book. The cover was a boy on a swing with no color. I opened the book and it turned out to be an ancient language. There were some pictures of a black cat with the little boy. There was an old fashioned stove, sink, and couch. The objects were all in one room. There were some brown stairs and when I went up them they creaked. There was a bed made out of hay with dirty sheets. There was a wooden shelf with a candle and a stray black cat with green eyes. It was the same black cat from the leather book! On the shelf where the black cat was sitting was a black cat and a white picture with the same black cat. The black cat was dirty and old. There was a wooden basket with an old doll inside it. I picked up the doll. The doll was wearing a pink dress. The doll had black hair. I set the doll back down in the woven basket. I looked at the black cat and thought *the cat looks really skinny*. I decided to feed it. So I went downstairs and went outside. I went to the store and got some cat food. Then I went to my house. I got water in a cup and food in a bowl. I went to the barn and went upstairs and gave the cat some food and water. The cat was eating and drinking fast, when I said, "Maybe I should give you a name."

Tavie Puklich, Grade 4
Hilltop Primary School, Minnetrista
Teaching Artist, Kelly Barnhill

A Climate Change Exchange

Global warming looms
Earth is doomed
New president
Isn't helping us anytime soon
And the people

Make me feel marooned
As if I'm a pirate
Stuck on an island
Without his crew

Trump thinks it's a hoax
By the Chinese
The other half of the nation disagrees
Though we all have a common enemy
Us uninvolved
Didn't ask to be born into this place
But alas
The human race
Shall be the last we wipe off the planet's face

And every time I'm reminded
My sense of urgency grows
It has even brought me
To new lows

Laying around
And getting selfish thoughts
"If they can delay it, I'll live a full life"
But I know they cannot
And I know that's a horrible way

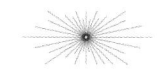

To leave behind my blood
And I'd rather watch the world flood

What if when
Someone couldn't get their work done on time
Boom Ice caps crashed
Forests burn to ash
It's too late to stop all the gas
Woosh Oceans flood
Drawing the planet's blood
Leaving it a place where no flowers could bud

But in this situation
The world's people are procrastinating
And it's about time we join together
To stop the useless waiting
To protect the world from devastation
To unite the people within our nation
We must rise up
To end this crisis
Because the state of the future of our planet
Is nothing short of priceless

Qais Stovall, Grade 8
Lake Harriet Upper School, Minneapolis
Teaching Artist, Frank Sentwali

Venezuela

Venezuela is part of my past
With the beautiful flamenco dance
With the chicha and arepa sense
With the yellow, blue and red
And the beautiful seven stars
This is me… the long skirt with the colors from the flag
And the baseball in the sky
With the marvelous sparkling waterfalls
I have respect from my country and for my people
Land and sea will be the one for me
This is me… representing my country
This is me… learning my language
This is me… a flag with seven reflecting stars

Susana Torrence, Grade 5
Royal Oaks Elementary School, Woodbury
Teaching Artist, Tou SaiKo Lee

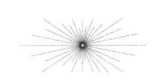

Caribbean Bracelet

gems of bright blue
but gray in the middle
from years
of being worn
like a lake
with cloudy waters

a band of gold
with scratches
and scars
wrapping around my wrist
like an old
snake
gently sleeping
in the trees

simple
but fancy
old
and worn
but when I wear it
it feels special
and new
reminding me
of the Caribbean Sea
and reminding me
of my Abuela

Samantha Fernandez, Grade 6
Oak View Middle School, Anoka
Teaching Artist, Susan Marie Swanson

Childhood

Let me tell you a story
Just a few weeks ago, I remembered 5th grade
And I thought, wow, times were easier back then
Almost no homework, only one teacher, and we didn't have to care about grades
So, I started thinking

We are children
We are young, opportunistic, open
Our stresses and problems are like kittens
Compared to the grizzly bears faced by adults
But many people don't understand
Exactly the value of this freedom

The privilege of our childhood,
To not need to work to survive
As children, our problems are so insignificant
We only get this point in our lives once
And some people aren't privileged enough to get it at all

We are among the luckiest people on Earth
To have a great education
And a great city, and great lives
So, what absolutely baffles me
Is why some people don't appreciate that

Many people don't seem to get
Exactly how quickly our youthful freedom will fade
How our carelessness and low-stress lives will degrade
We're already starting to lose this freedom, here in 8th grade

With constant bombardments of drafts to write
And maps to analyze
And packets to fill out
And spoken word poems to memorize
Bang bang bang bang bang bang bang, the assignments come rapid-fire!

Now, I'm not saying these things aren't stressful
But the workload will only get harder from here!
These kittens we're facing are already growing into lions
So, my message is a request if anything
Please, make the most of every last second of your free time
Because high school?
College?
An actual job?
None of those things are going to be easy
The most stressful of times have yet to come

So, the next time you're stressed
The next time you're hopelessly behind schedule
The next time you're trying to fall asleep when you realize you have an essay due tomorrow,
Just remember
You'll get through it
The sun will still rise
Our grades don't even matter yet
So please, try to realize
Our cozy kitten life is limited
So make the most of it
Because we are only children

Max Opitz, Grade 8
South View Middle School, Edina
Teaching Artist, Frank Sentwali

Working on a Building

Going to wake up in the morning
Working on a building
Going to dig a hole, down in the ground
Going to wake up in the morning
Working on a building
Going to put up walls, all around

And when it's done, it'll be beautiful
Working on a building all around

Going to wake up in the morning
Working in a factory
Going to work hard, all day long
Going to wake up in the morning
Working in a factory
Making things, good and strong

And when we're done, it'll be beautiful
Working in a factory all day long

Going to wake up in the morning
Going to write a song for you
Going to take my pen, and write it down
Going to wake up in the morning
Going to write a song for you
That will make you happy
And won't make you frown

And when we're done, it'll be beautiful
Going to make you happy, all day long

Mr. Terrones' Class, Kindergarten
Saint Anthony Park Elementary School, Saint Paul
Teaching Artist, Charlie Maguire

Section 4:
Finding New Forms

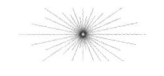

Don't Trash Me

Don't trash me
or else all my lead will fall
      out

Don't rip my eraser
      'cause then
you can't mess up anymore
(We both know you do that
      a lot)

Don't sharpen my head or else
there will be nothing
      left to write with
(Plus I don't want to be any
shorter than I already am)

If you do sharpen me
(Which you shouldn't have even
done in the first place)
don't leave my shavings
      everywhere!

      STOP!

You're hurting me now
      FIX IT!

Sarah Bagley, Grade 5
Creek Valley Elementary School, Edina
Teaching Artist, Becca Barniskis

If My Pen Was a Magic Wand

If my pen was a magic wand
I would be Hermione Granger
I would walk the halls of Hogwarts
With power
I would know how to
Make an apple into a pineapple
Using my wand that's how
And plus
Everyone would give her a bow
If my pen
Was a magic wand
Then I would have so
So many flowers
Because my pen would have
Magical powers
I would make the world
A better place
Just because I like to retrace
My steps
I would swoosh my pen
And all the homeless and lost
Would find homes
I would twirl my pen
Like a dancer does to their ribbon
And all the starving would find simply superb super silly
Meals
Sometimes even
My pen would find the good in the bad
Bad people
My pen would only do good
If it got into the wrong hands

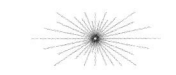

It would demand
It would demand to be given back to me
If my pen had magical powers
That's why soon
The whole world would be a better place
Just because
The world should be an amazing place
Where people give back
To the less fortunate
Well
My pen would make it that way
I'd clean
Up the streets
By saying one word
"Clean"
The world
Doesn't need a
Magic pen it only needs
You, me and many
Kindhearted people
Oh
And maybe one or two
Kindhearted squirrels

Signe Elftmann, Grade 5
Hillcrest Community School, Bloomington
Teaching Artist, Frank Sentwali

A Day in the Life of Ferox

This is EOS, a land of prosperity and opputunities. That cottage on that little hill over there is where I live with my mother. It looks bleak, but trust me, it's great!

So, let me show you what usually happens in a day for me, and maybe some things about me.

Firstly, after I wake up, I eat some breakfast. A nine-teen year old of course needs his food every morning!

Then I go outside to tend to the magnolia plants. I really enjoy gardening these types of flowers. There's something that makes it special!

Magnolia plants are healing agents, which is why they're so important to the witch bloodline. My mother Nora, who is the witch of EOS, says that they are sacred and are only gifted to those with the blood of a witch. Many citizens have visited to purchase these flowers.

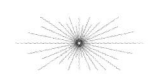

Later, I'll go out to the city to hang out with friends from school... maybe a bit of shopping, too.
AHH!
I'll get back home, and that's when I have to practice my powers with Mother. It's SO hard to try to control it without causing an explosion of some sort.
It's frustrating to the point where I'd give up completely. I cannot make any mistakes anymore. I'd basically humiliate the power and persistence my ancestors had.
But... my mom always encourages me no matter what. She's the one who keeps pushing me forward.
MAGNUS
I also have to go back inside to pray to my grandmother, Magnus. She was an excellent witch who served the King.
Magnus
Nora
ME
Grandmother was the one who helped Mother when Father passed away. I certainly respected her back then. My family line had been so diligent while I seemed to be a "mess-up".

L. P., Grade 8
North View Middle School, Brooklyn Park
Teaching Artist, Fiona Avocado

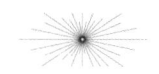

Recipe for: Everyone

From the kitchen of: Karina Hydrie
Prep time: 30 minutes
Cook time: 1 hour
Serves: ∞

Ingredients:
- 2 cups of courage
- a handful of uniqueness
- an imagination
- 1+ friends to believe in you
- Heaps of understanding
- 4 cups of sugar
- 2 medium-sized bowls
- 1 bundt pan

Directions:
Preheat oven to 375°F
1. Take your 4 cups of sugar and 2 cups of courage and put them in a medium-sized bowl. Mix well and then put the bowl aside.
2. With the other medium-sized bowl, put in a handful of uniqueness, your 1+ friends to believe in you and an imagination. Put in mixer for 10 minutes
3. Take both your bowls and mix them together for 5-10 minutes.
4. Pour it into the bundt pan and bake it for 20 minutes or until cake tester comes out clean. Take it out and let it cool for 10 minutes. Enjoy!

Karina Hydrie, Grade 5
Capitol Hill Gifted and Talented Magnet, Saint Paul
Teaching Artist, T. Mychael Rambo

Recipe for: Do You, Be You, Be-you-ti-ful

From the kitchen of: Lucy Dosch
Prep time: 6 ½ minutes
Cook time: 30 minutes
Serves: Everyone

Ingredients:
- 2 cups of originality
- a sprinkle of attitude
- 2 ½ cups of truth
- 1 tsp of happiness
- 1 gallon of yourself
- ½ cup of outstanding
- 1 tbsp. of laughter
- a dash of sweetness
- 3 handfuls of imagination

Directions:
Put 2 cups of originality, 2 ½ cups of truth and 1 gallon of yourself in a bowl and mix for 1 minute. In a different bowl, mix ½ cup of outstanding, 1 tbsp. of laughter, a dash of sweetness, 3 handfuls of imagination and a sprinkle of attitude for 1 ½ minutes. Pour the two bowls together and mix for 4 minutes. Pour the mixture into a 4" x 11" pan then put it into the oven at 180° for 30 minutes. Take out when ready and serve it to everyone you wish.

Lucy Dosch, Grade 5
Capitol Hill Gifted and Talented Magnet, Saint Paul
Teaching Artist, T. Mychael Rambo

Six-Word Memoirs:

1. After it rains there's a rainbow
2. Being alone, I'm my own soldier
3. Don't trust many people, they're snakes
4. Want to explore, but no money
5. Crystal clear water, I'm pure, too

Gabrianna Vasquez, Grade 11
Edison High School, Minneapolis
Teaching Artist, Alexei Moon Casselle

Being a Princess Is Not So Great

V. P. G., Grade 8
North View Middle School, Brooklyn Park
Teaching Artist, Fiona Avocado

The Scooter

A person on a scooter that has body armor, football helmet, thick knee/leg pads, football shoulder pads, big boots and big goggles.

Characters: Ben and Dree
Setting: Alley

Ben: Hey Dree!! Come out here.
Dree: What do you want?
Ben: You said you need something to "ride" right?
Dree: Yeah, what did you get me, a mot…
Ben: A scooter!
Dree: …Really…a scooter…
Ben: But hey it goes really fast!
Dree: It looks all trashy and rusty and in bad condition.
Ben: It's fine…here's all the safety gear, I got you a football helmet, thick knee and elbow pads, body armor, big thick goggles, shoulder pads, steel filled in boots, samurai amour, safety glasses, a mouth guard, a bottom mouth guard, a chin pad…it's metal, ear plugs, toilet paper, and a super thick jacket.
Dree: Okay, thanks.
Ben: You're welcome.
Dree: I can barely walk in this, it's so heavy.
Ben: Okay, start the scooter.
Dree: OMG!!!
Ben: What?
Dree: The keys, where are the keys?
Ben: Oops, I think I put it into one of the safety gear pieces…
Dree: You got to be kidding me! I got to take this all off now?

One and a half hours later…

Dree: (tired) haaaa, I'm bushed. Okay, where is it? (looking for it)
Ben: Oh! Hey I found it. The key…
Dree: Okay then let's start it up! (Starts scooter). The key doesn't fit.
Ben: Wait this key is for this (lock on the scooter). Now try this.
Dree: Okay, it still doesn't fit.
Ben: No, no, no…it's for this lock.
Dree: This one! (Click, opens second lock).
Ben: The next lock.
Dree: OMG, how many locks?
Ben: About 15, then a dead bolt lock, then a combination lock. (16 locks later).
Dree: Okay, what's the combination?
Ben: I don't know.
Dree: Hey, when did you get a tattoo?
Ben: Oh, this is just numbers.

Muajtsim (TJ) Yang, Grade 8
North View Middle School, Brooklyn Park
Teaching Artist, Levi Weinhagen

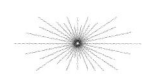

Energy: History/Consequences/Solutions

<u>OPENING</u>

Ozone traps heat into the earth's atmosphere
It sounds like glass shattering
Tastes like black exhaust coming through your vents

Crashing atoms
You are trapped and you have no escape
People wheezing and gasping for at least one breath of fresh air
Water rising the rushing water of a melting glacier

Smells like old eggs

Cracking icebergs starting to fall
Blue skies turning dark gray

Darkness inside dirty air
Trash clogs the river
Destruction for cities and towns

A hurricane
A big fire full of electrons
A thousand bombs falling at once
Zeus' tongue striking down thunder storms

Unhealthy air that irritates my throat
A blanket of smog thrown over my head
Dusty clouds

Radiation is energy that doesn't stop
Looks like nobody is doing anything about it
Never take it for granted

ICE CAPS MELTING

ALL
Good evening we are coming to you live from CNN.

BRIDGET AND MAYA
Today we will be talking to you about the ice caps melting in the North Pole.

ALL
The Arctic Circle.

OBI AND CARSON
Here in the North Pole, showing you the local glaciers that are melting

LUKE AND DUSTY
And you most likely won't see them in 2023.

CARSON, DUSTY, LUKE
Fun fact: The North Pole is just floating ice. Not land.

OBI AND MAYA
There's a lot of carbon dioxide in the atmosphere

LUKE AND DUSTY
From cars and planes.

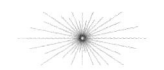

ALL
Factories,
The burning of fossil fuels,

BRIDGET, DUSTY, CARSON
Makes greenhouse gases

OBI, MAYA, LUKE
That trap heat into the Earth's

ALL
Atmosphere.

BRIDGET, DUSTY, CARSON
Too much heat.

OBI, MAYA, LUKE
Way more than normal.

BRIDGET, DUSTY, CARSON
So the glaciers are melting,

OBI, MAYA, LUKE
And the seas are rising.

MAYA, BRIDGET, OBI AND CARSON
You can also see the cute Polar Bear cubs. Their Mom and Dad are probably out looking for food.

DUSTY AND LUKE
Polar Bears hunt for sea lions on ice.

ALL
And the ice is melting!

SMOG

ELIAS AND JAYDEN
Happy to see you back today. We'll be covering smog.

ALL
What is smog?

ELIAS AND JAYDEN
Smoke.

CAYDEN GRACE ETHAN MIKODA
Fog.

ALL
Smog.

CAYDEN AND GRACE
We're here with two Minneapolis residents, both with asthma.

ELIAS AND JAYDEN
I hear air pollution sends 1,000 people in Minneapolis to the hospital a year.

MIKODA AND ETHAN
I spend as much time as I can indoors. I cough and wheeze.

ALL
What causes smog?

GRACE AND MIKODA
Air pollution.

ALL
What causes air pollution?

ELIAS AND JAYDEN
Car exhaust,

CAYDEN AND ETHAN
Coal power plants,

GRACE
Factory emissions.

<u>RECYCLE</u>

Brennen and Carter take a long drink from their bottles of pop and walk along and throw plastic bottles in front of them (but not into the audience). They walk and are followed by the other actors.

BRENNEN AND CARTER
Why are you following us?

PAYTON, EMMA, NOVALEE, SAWYER
Because you're littering.

CARTER AND BRENNEN
So what?

SAWYER
Did you know that there is

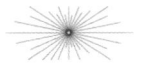

PAYTON
15,110,000,000 pounds

EMMA AND NOVALEE
Of trash in the USA thrown away

SAWYER AND PAYTON
Every year?

BRENNER AND CARTER
Who cares?

SAWYER AND NOVALEE AND PAYTON AND EMMA
An animal could eat your trash and die.

BRENNEN AND CARTER
Who cares.

NOVALEE AND EMMA
Garbage can be toxic.

SAWYER AND NOVALEE AND PAYTON
But if you put your garbage in the trash

PAYTON AND EMMA
Or recycling

SAWYER AND NOVALEE AND PAYTON
It can get reused!

BRENNEN AND CARTER
Reused?

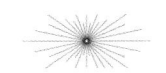

SAWYER AND NOVALEE AND PAYTON
Made into something new. Or turned into electricity.

BRENNEN AND CARTER
How?

SAWYER AND NOVALEE
The garbage decays in the landfill.

PAYTON AND EMMA
It produces methane gas.

SAWYER AND NOVALEE
Lutheran Hospital uses that to heat their building in Onalaska.

PAYTON AND EMMA
Trash is also burned

SAWYER AND NOVALEE
To heat water that creates steam

PAYTON EMMA SAWYER NOVALEE
That turns the turbines

SAWYER NOVALEE PAYTON EMMA
Biomass!

BRENNEN AND CARTER
Biomass…

EMMA
There's a biomass plant right near here

PAYTON AND SAWYER
On French Island.

(Brennen and Carter pick up their plastic bottles.)

CLOSING

Energy moves everything we do.
It feels like power.
It sounds like wind or the buzzing from a bee.

Wind creates energy.
Biomass comes from my trash.

Electricity is best made renewable.

Nature is precious,
Enlighten our world.
Energy is you, it created you.

Mrs. Reichgelt's Class, Grade 6
La Crescent-Hokah Middle School, La Crescent
Teaching Artist, Taous Khazem

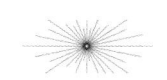

Section 5:
What Life Throws at Us

I Am the One

Have you heard
Your parents sob?
Have you heard
A heart scream and throb?
Have you seen
the moment someone's life turns around
like a top on its turn,
the moment someone's life stops chugging up the hill
and starts rolling down
tumbling down
hurtling down that hill?

I have, and I am the one.
I am the one who threw myself in front of the boulder
not knowing that the only option
was to keep trying to push it up that hill
or get crushed
crippled
and crumbled under its weight.
Because the weight was too much
and the pain ripped through my muscles…
Slice…
and there wasn't enough air to suffice.

In that moment I decided to be the rock
be the one who everyone THINKS is strong.
But I am weak
and the only thing that truly knows how weak I am
is my pillow
at night
as it soaks up my tears.

But I can't quit my job
of being the rock, I can't let the boulder fall
because I am the Sisyphus of the real world.
But this is not my punishment.
This is my reality.
This is my strength training.
This is how I keep hope for the future.

I am the one.
I am the one who threw myself in front of the boulder
because of that people THINK I am strong
but I am weak.
Yet as my arms tremble under the weight I rise
Because I love being a rock
I love being sturdy.
I love that people think I am strong.

Because after so many hours
days, months and months
of my hands pressing
pushing
and pursuing
that boulder getting it up that hill
I have become part of the boulder
my hands shooting roots into seems
my hands becoming crusted
crackled
and gray just like the boulder I hold in my hands.
Just like the life I have the power to destroy
just like the family that could crumble
just like the love I have the time to cherish

I learn how to handle the weight.
I learn how to turn from 13 to 31 on my birthday.
And even though the weight may never be lifted
I will persevere.
I will grow
and I will always have hope in my heart.
I am the one.
I am the one who threw myself in front of the boulder.
I may be weak sometimes
but I will be strong always.

Hannah Myers, Grade 8
South View Middle School, Edina
Teaching Artist, Frank Sentwali

Semi-Iceberg

I'm an iceberg, we're all icebergs.
Two meanings but they still mean the same.
Something happened to the kingdom of hope 'cause it was just left hanging at the end of the rope.
I think we're sinking from the thinking, these linking mostly shrinking two old worlds are taking apart my heart, show me true art of surviving to the end.
You can break my bones and tear my skin, but you will never ever take my friends.
You see, I once knew this boy who couldn't make the choice either to lie or cry, he couldn't define 'cause he didn't have the time to defy his own lies as he shouted up to the sky.
He taught me something important that day, that there's more inside.
He watched all the couples hug and walk down the same hill almost every day, he now lays in a coffin hidden in a scary place.
And going back to the kingdom of hope, I see a sea of kingdoms that can't even cope with their own doom.
I see you tearing down all the walls inside my room.
And tell me why every time I go to bed that's when my thoughts come alive and make me feel dead.
Kids aiming guns to their heads and when the knife collides with the skin, it's as easy as cutting a loaf of bread.
You say you wanna cut your wrists, but how can you when there's guns on your fist?
Maybe you can fix it with a kiss, this ain't a lovers' tryst.
I can't find the words that can fit.
And it's messed up how schools don't do anything about it, 'cause remember September's the month when the killer delivers the thriller to the sinner or winner

And that's all on us, nobody cares about you, 'cause we're all thrown under the bus.
We're just like dirt 'cause we're always getting stepped on causing fires in our minds yeah, look at the outcome.
How can you imprison the prisoners when you gotta assassinate the senator, clean up on aisle 16 cause we're just the janitors.
Analytically I will fight for what's right.
Metaphorically the dead will come alive tonight.
There's a million reasons why you shouldn't cry and try to fight for your own life.
We cut ourselves everyday but just in different ways.
My dreams are killing me now, this isn't a phase.
'Cause we're connected to life, just a bunch of semi-trucks.
We're all dying here but yet no one gives a f—
I'm sorry.
Pardon my language, I just got angry at the world there.
Let the evil be vanquished.
I once knew this girl, sometimes her dad would come home to bring her a "surprise."
I know some kids had it worse, but they're also taking their lives.
But what can I do, I'm just a kid.
Memories are on the brink of extinction and I don't know what I did.
Go ahead and scare us, trying to reach Heaven above.
But remember there's one thing that conquers all, and that's love.

Michaelsan Her, Grade 7
Community of Peace Academy, Saint Paul
Teaching Artist, Frank Sentwali

Ruined Childhood

As soon as I **step** in I can feel the **eyes**
Staring into my soul
Where this girl lay with depression and anxiety
Feeling so alone that tears just
Fall, even from **thinking** and **talking** about how she feels

I asked, are you okay?
She says to me when the happy people
Cry, everyone cries
Then she asks
Do you think I'm a happy person?
I say to her
No
I know, it's **fake**

Hidden by the fake smile
She bottles it all up
'Cause she can **never trust**
Anyone
She cries herself to sleep

Text me, call me when you need me
Of course, I needed you
But **where are you now that I need you: POOF**
Gone

When it comes to the love from a father
It's even worse

Love live laugh
How can we love? When we're born into

War, raised to be child soldiers
Never had a **full stomach**
Never felt **real love**
Taught to hold and fire a **gun**
Taught to wear a vest and **run**

How can I live?
When I'm on the front line
When I stand facing a gun to my head

How can I laugh?
I don't even smile
All I hear are cries and shots being fired
Look into the eyes of a child soldier
You can see the **tears**
Filled with **fear**
Will it ever end?

Htoo Eh Say, Grade 8
Humboldt Senior High School, Saint Paul
Teaching Artist, Frank Sentwali

I Should Have Stayed in Bed Today

I should have stayed in bed today
In bed's where I belong
As soon as I got up today
Things started going wrong
I got a splinter in my foot
My puppy made me fall
I squirted toothpaste in my ear
I crashed into the wall

        I knocked my homework off the desk
        It landed on my toes
        I spilled a glass of chocolate milk
        It's soaking through my clothes
        I accidentally bit my tongue
        That really made me moan
        And it was far from funny
        When I banged my funny bone

I scraped my knees, I bumped my nose
I sat upon a pin
I leapt up with alacrity
And sharply banged my eye
The pain is quite severe
I'd better get right back to bed
And stay there for a year

S. C., Grade 9
Roosevelt High School, Minneapolis
Teaching Artist, Frank Sentwali

My Life Lived

I was born after a flood
Of loss
In a storm
Of once

The fifth of ten or
The third of eight

Little houses
Little thoughts
It all goes away
Big house
Better yard
Bigger intentions

After this sudden change
My thoughts
Are never
Quiet

Death was accepted
For there was nothing else to do

Can YOU erase death?
Pretend it didn't happen?

School was close enough
To touch
Then it moved
It shifted
Further away from me

My emotions can
Change
Wane
Grow
Like any others
Mad and Angry can be controlled
Sad and Depressed are harder
Happy and Joyous are loved and accepted
Normal and Neutral are never recognized

My work is
Hard
Gardening
Chores
Siblings
School

But I cannot complain
I would spring the mouse's trap

Plans
Ideas
Expansion
Those are in my head

I love
Reading
Dancing
Music
Nature
My siblings
(Though I do get angry
And wish

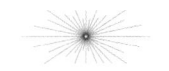

That I could be an only child
But it's impossible)

I was born of
Laughter
And Joy
And Love
And friends

And family

My pets, any pets
Or animals
Pets are friends
Companions
Angels
In the bodies of our favorite animals;
Cats
Hamsters
Fish
Turtles
Birds

But sadly
Losses follow

Nature is
Peaceful
A break from the world
(And my family
I have to breathe
On occasion)
It makes me Happy

And Loved
Nature is gorgeous
Loved by artists
And me, an artist too
Among so many
Negatives
Or positives
Which are best for me?

Homemade goodies
Are made
By loving hands
Tenderly and
Carefully
Made just for children

At least thirteen years
Of experience
Learned or made into lessons
Or wasted
Or chosen and cherished
Followed or
Ignored
Or heeded
Loved
Or forgotten
Like a warm summer day
Or that song you really love

Sadness came after
Gold
It turns to
Silver

Then Bronze
Iron
Might replace all
It is a strong support
I cannot deny that
But it can still be defeated

I am always
Writing of adventures
Creating everything within my reach
Making treats and Love, and friendships
Dreaming about the future and my plans
Raining my emotions into droplets
Storming, because a cloud does need to get Angry
Dancing so hard I cannot stop
Laughing because it's natural
Playing, so that I feel like a child again
Sleeping until noon is my wish (which is impossible in my family)
Bored so badly in math

Singing along with my songs
Hoping that we can live in Harmony
Helping everyone who needs a service done
Eating, because I'm crazy about food
Living life
Loving someone
Holding somebody in my dreams
Watching that person
Together

Can this
All of this
Be my future,
And my past?
It's too much to hope for
So I'll wish
On a star
I wish (or hope)
That Love
Overthrows
Iron
Gold
Will replace it
And it will never fail

Some ends
Must be tied
Before they break
Or they must be replaced
Or kept

And now I believe
That you (Yes, you!) can make a difference
The difference that splashes
In the pond
Of life
It will make ripples
But it shouldn't destroy
And everyone can reach their full extent
Of life
(Or love)

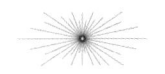

Don't despair
Because after storms
Rainbows appear
And after night
Day comes
Before dark
Sunset
Then sunrise

This is my story
My experiences
My explanation
My life
Read it
Keep it
Love it
Well

Daisy Johnstun, Grade 7
Roseau Secondary School, Roseau
Teaching Artist, Rachel Moritz

It Was Fine

It was just us three.
Big brother, you and me.
   And it was fine.
We enjoyed life as a family.
   And that was fine.
We all stuck together
Like a pb & jelly sandwich.
   And it was fine.
You wanted me to meet someone
   And it was fine.
He made you act like a sweet innocent bunny to a vicious jaguar going in for the kill
But… it was fine.
He made me hate you
And made me leave but…
   It was fine.
I always kept my emotions away from the world and
   … it was… I can't take it anymore.
It's not fine that you change for another being that has a relationship
Status that says butler and master.
   It's not ok that you let me bleed inside.
All the pain he gave me.
It's not fine.
That you treated my brother like a broken puppet that's no use to anyone.
That is not fine.
Now you tell me, mother
Is losing the people who love you the most, fine?!
You tell me?!

Elliot Tuck, Grade 8
White Bear Middle School, White Bear Lake
Teaching Artist, SEE MORE PERSPECTIVE

Come Aboard the Train of Pain

An incurable disease.
The victim driving his own train of pain and loss, tearing apart the fabric of his beloved family, the express line to a land of forgotten faces, lost skills, derailed plans for the future.
Lost, off the tracks.
Alzheimer's, dazing off at the end of a tunnel.
Every mile he goes, brings in deeper.
He can't control what is messing with his brain.
A runaway train, faster than superman can fly.
Still he's fighting, calling out for a superhero that isn't coming.
There is no cure.
The track splits, he is lost in confusion, he doesn't know which lever to pull.
There are flashing lights, mixed signals, blinded with confusion, the lever he wants to pull does not match the map.
Every city he goes under, the tunnel darkens towards the end.
More worries, illusions of turns, tension in his brain.
This is a one way track.
There is no cure.
Caregivers, riding along a train they did not buy a ticket for, and loved ones, helplessly standing there watching from the station, looking at this train wreck, as it chugs along.
A train wreck caused by no fault of the engineer.
The engineer doesn't even realize the disease, except for a heavy feeling of unease, and fear that something is not quite right.
The passengers know what is at the end of the tunnel, but they can't get off the train either.

The train of thought losing cars on its way to the end of the tunnel.

What was said from the radio, and what was heard, has just been forgotten, like memories being washed down the drain.

Being carried by the aged water that was once alive, and flowing.

The train is not turning back now.

The cars are long gone in his past.

There is no turning back, there is no more learning.

Once he starts he can't stop.

Going 200 miles an hour, he tries to slam on the brakes, but they don't work.

There is no cure.

Bending his mind, and refocusing his brain, to find the next thought.

He is focused on pressing random buttons, because he's not sure what to do, where to go, or how to call Superman to come save the day.

Watching as the world he is forgetting, forgets him.

Trying to slam on the brakes, so he does not reach the end of the tunnel.

Alzheimer's.

An incurable disease.

Annelise Daniels, Grade 7
Oak Hill Montessori School, Shoreview
Teaching Artist, Desdamona

I Wish

I wish that every time I've said next time, I should've said this time.
And instead of saying no it's okay, I should've said yes it's fine.
Sadly since you're not here now,
I watched myself wished a wish
as if I was a little girl again, on my bed, on my knees, on my hands wishing again.
I wish that when I was only five minutes away I would have stopped by,
But no I said you should be fine without seeing me stand by your side.

Whispering "hello," as if I was putting a baby to sleep.
He's gone.
Choking, crying, shuttering
stop lying.
Thoughts running through my mind just like a moth to a flame, running, flying directly into the flame hoping it was a light that led me to a lie.
Time has stopped running down this rocky road,
I closed my eyes, 6:45 AM.
I'm awake, are you okay? No, I'm not duh it's like
asking a man who was stabbed 50 times if he was fine.
I opened my phone and read.
He said please don't cry, I couldn't help it a waterfall came running out of my eyes.
Oh the pain
Two weeks later I got on the plane,
my heart, my mind, my thoughts were flying somewhere else.
I wish that this wasn't true I wish that this was all a lie,

next thing I knew I was already stepping into row A32.
LANDED.
LAX.
Arrived, a small town, an Asian house, 50 cars or more parked around the house, on an empty land. My aunts came rushing out,
sleeping silently softly on his bed.
Tissues, tears, time has stopped once more.
Maybe this time my heart.
Three days passed you were being put away; I was so close to being pulled away.
I whispered "give him this flower for me."
I walked away, I hugged my father and he said,
"He won't be around anymore, but he will always be here."
Tears were there, crying for three days straight, with four hours of sleep each day.
Tears weren't coming anymore.
It's like being stabbed without bleeding.
I opened the backseat door; I sank like an anchor into my seat.
Back to LAX,
FLIGHT to Minneapolis is boarding.
12 AM, midnight, into seat B13 this time.
I looked outside and cried over the clouds, a small voice came calling out.
"We're going to be in the sky like grandpa now…"
I looked for the brightest star shining in the sky,
I was so close to getting up and flying.
I closed my eyes,
I put my hands together and said I wished,
I wish for one last goodbye. I wish next lifetime you will still be here next to me. I wish that even when the sky is falling you will be standing, you're a hero stronger than any

superhero. I wish that you watch over me wonderfully and that I'm still a princess in your eye.
I just wish one last wish.

Kathy Gao Ia Yang, Grade 11
Humboldt Senior High School, Saint Paul
Teaching Artist, Frank Sentwali

Fear Starts with C

As an English student who knows sign language, I am obsessed with the alphabet.
Letters make words and words make a vignette.
But, to me, the scholars who made these words got some wrong.
As the letters themselves don't always seem to truly belong.

For example, as you can clearly see
Fear starts with the letter C.
C as in a claustrophobic cockroach community,
or as in a chaotic cause of calamity.

I write alliteration to make myself chuckle time after time
like a despicable crook after he just committed a vile crime.
But I only commit to writing,
because it's extremely difficult to stop crying.

I notice you all glaring at me, like I'm just some crazy.
It's ok to stare. Since the diagnosis, my mind has gotten hazy.
Don't worry, I'll tell my story. However, it still gives me issues.
If any of you are sensitive, then try to grab some tissues.

It's 11:40 AM in the doctor's room and I just had a pudding cup for an early lunch.
The nurse walks in with a folder and I have this dreadful hunch.
She sits down and tells me this prolonged answer,
and the silly thing is that I don't remember what she said other than four words:

Stage III heart cancer.
Like most people, I just denied it. It couldn't be true.
I had no idea that it was there. To know it was in me, I never knew.
I see you all staring. Like I said, I'm a freak.
But just because I have cancer, doesn't mean I'm weak.

What I've noticed when you say cancer is that people give you looks.
It's interesting seeing their expressions because I can read them like books.
Some show of pity and some show fear.
Some are showing that they just can't hide away that one single tear.

There's just something with those scholars I can't say I can agree.
For you see, fear doesn't begin with an F, but it starts with a C.
C as in cancer. An illness that kills people and breaks families apart.
And before I knew it, I am what seems to be the start.

But all I can really say is that fear starts with C.
The C for cancer that stings you like a bee.
They think they know words, well let's see.
I want to see what they think when they look at me.

Why do bad things happen to good people? That is a question I ask myself often.
Because I don't know if you know this, but I really can't picture myself in a coffin.

I don't mean to scare you and I don't want to make you cry.
I just need to say the truth… I am going to die.

Skyllar Schoening, Grade 9
Roseau Secondary School, Roseau
Teaching Artist, Frank Sentwali

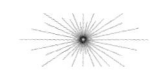

Never

Well I'm not good at singing,
and I could never let go.
But if there is something that I know, my feeling will never get old.
You could drag me up to Heaven,
or drag me down to Hell.
But no matter what, I will not give up, 'cause I'm not letting go.
I would take a bullet
for all those I love.
You could pull the trigger and I'd just snicker, 'cause I'm not letting go.

There's a big ole world out here,
and I really love this place,
so c'mon man and take my hand, please just try to keep pace.

Oh I have taken damage,
of each and every kind,
but listen here and let's be dear, a heart break could bring fear.
You can hate me all you want now,
And that is A okay,
but no matter what I will not give up, 'cause I'm not letting go.

Letting go, letting go
I'll be trudging through the snow, in a negative gust, of frozen dust, but I will still be there.

You can say all of those mean things,
you can swear that you're okay,
but I'll always care so don't you dare say that you are simply just ok.

I have heard each and every lie,
all on multiple times,
and I know your heart even though you thought, that I was not there.
That's all inconvenience, because I know I was, but no matter what, I will not give up, 'cause I'm not letting go.

Letting go, letting go
walking over hot coals, blisters on my feet and oh!
Now don't you mind, you're one of a kind, and pain will subside.

There's a big ole beautiful sky,
and there's the deep black sea,
but there's this place that takes up space just in between.
I have all my faith in you
and everything you can do,
because no matter what I will not give up, 'cause I'm not letting go.

N. E., Grade 11
Brainerd Area Education Center, Brainerd
Teaching Artist, Saymoukda Vongsay

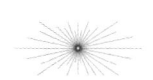

Section 6:
Diving into Adventure

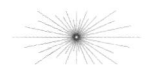

One Beautiful Thing

The sun was shining on this late fall day. Emily's uncle was lying in bed coughing. Emily went into his room to get him ready for work. Right away, she knew he wouldn't be able to go to work.

He seemed very sick. His face was pale, he was sweating and his body was full of pain. Emily knew that this was a bad illness. In fact, her mother had died from it just three years ago. She couldn't go to the doctor in town because it was too far. With all of the dangers on the road, they both might as well die. Emily zoomed to her aunt's room to tell her the news.

Emily's aunt told her that she had a way to cure the illness. Emily's aunt was very wise. She had been alive for seventy years, which was a long time to live in the 1700s. Emily's aunt told Emily to go get special things for her uncle. Here was the list she got:

1. The tiniest egg in a sparrow's nest;
2. A cup of fresh rainfall; and
3. One beautiful thing.

Those things were impossible but, to save her uncle, Emily had to try.

First thing: the egg of a sparrow. Emily threw on her jacket and walked out the door, not looking forward to her adventure ahead. As she was walking, she heard the small sound of a sparrow's call. She ran toward the sound. She saw the nest high in the tree. Emily already felt defeated. How in the world could she get to the nest—it was so high. She looked at the ground and spotted a rock. She picked up the rock, gripped it in her hand and threw. The rock hit the edge of the nest. But it did nothing to it. She needed something bigger.

Next, she saw a stone. "This would work," she thought. She threw and hit it! The nest came tumbling down. Emily ran to catch it. She caught the nest. She looked into the nest and pulled out the smallest egg. It was as big as her handheld pencil sharpener. She put the egg in her pocket and ran away, knowing she didn't have a lot of time. The sun was going down and she still had two things on the list.

Emily was walking, keeping her eyes peeled for the second thing on the list. This one was going to be hard! It hardly rained in the place where she lived. But, to her surprise, as she was walking she stepped in a freshly made puddle. She pulled out her cup and scooped up the water. "Two down and one to go," she thought. "One beautiful thing?" Emily said. She didn't understand. "Beauty means different things to different people."

Suddenly, Emily knew what she had to do. "I need to get one of everything I think is beautiful. But even if I don't think it's beautiful, I will still get it." She was getting tired. Judging from the darkness around her, she figured it was about 7:00 in the evening. But she still had to get the One Beautiful Thing. It was going to be easy and hard. So much beauty in nature, but such little time to get it all.

However, Emily had a feeling about what she wanted. First things first, she needed something she thought was beautiful.

The first thing Emily got was a maple leaf. Emily chose that particular item because she could remember sitting outside and admiring all the beautiful colors of the leaves. She put it in her pocket and as she heard the crunch of the leaf, she again realized that there were too many beautiful things in the world and she could never get them all. Sad and disappointed, Emily ran back to her house, the wind blowing in her face and teardrops falling to the ground. She opened the door to her house and started bawling to her aunt about what happened.

"Now he will never survive," Emily said with her chin trembling.

"Yes, he will!" Emily's aunt exclaimed.

"But I didn't finish the list."

Emily's aunt looked at her, smiled and said, "You are the only one who can heal him. Only people who know the true meaning of beauty can."

"I don't understand," said Emily, with confusion in her voice.

"I was trying to see if you could see beauty in everything and you can."

Emily looked at her stunned, her eyes bugging out of her head.

"What are you staring at me for?" said Emily's aunt. "Go heal him."

"Okay," said Emily.

Emily went into her uncle's room and touched his pale, freezing hand. As she touched him, she felt the warmth of life come back into his body. Her uncle opened his eyes, just barely, and was able to say only seven words:

"You did it. You are truly beautiful."

Emily hugged her uncle, with beautiful feelings overflowing out of her.

Emily always remembered what her aunt said to her, even in her last moment. She knew the true meaning of beauty and she would never forget it.

Elizabeth Ekman, Grade 5
Meadowbrook Elementary School, Golden Valley
Teaching Artist, Stephen Peters

Almost Average

School was out in five minutes and I was excited. We were learning about the human body, which was super boring. Finally—3, 2, 1, BEEB! That bell is so annoying but it makes me happy.

I'm a regular straight A student, same schedule every day: wake up at 8:00 AM, eat breakfast, go to school, ride my bike home, eat dinner, do homework, go to bed.

But on my way home that day I took a different route thinking it would be faster. It worked but I saw these two sixth graders on their bikes stopped and talking to each other. When I passed them, they said "Hey!" But I just ignored them. They wouldn't stop trying, though. They yelled and asked, "Do you wanna have some fun?"

I slowly came to a stop and turned around and said, "What kind of fun?" They said they were going to go steal some copper from the old school the community was tearing down and turning into a grocery store. I knew better than that so I made up this cheesy excuse. I said I had a lot of homework, which wasn't a full lie because I had my math test the next day. But they said they would pay me $50 and THAT was my weak side. Immediately I said, "Yeah, sure!"

So there I was going to an abandoned school, stealing, doing one of the most done crimes. I kind of trusted them and I brightened up a bit, but when we got to the school, it looked like my whole city was in this place. I saw cars everywhere. One of the sixth graders, Tim, said everybody was leaving work and it would die down later.

As we went inside the school the other sixth grader, Alex, said, "Grab as much as you can. The more we take, the more money!" A smirk grew on my face. I started ripping, tearing, having a blast. About a half hour later I asked if we were done. We agreed we had enough.

When I got home I felt like an idiot. I was so guilty and of course I lied to my mom's face. I said I tried another way home but got lost. She hugged me and kissed me and I still felt awful. I probably would have gotten grounded for a month if my mom found out what I did.

The next day the sixth graders gave me the money they got from my copper and my $50 for doing something so bad. After school I took the same route and of course the sixth graders were there. They offered me the same deal, but I DEFINITELY wasn't interested. I kept on biking and so did they. I went faster and so did they. They were chasing me and this was getting out of hand! I wasn't sure which way to go, but then I saw my friend Jake and I tried to yell but he couldn't hear me.

Then a rock in the path flipped me up and onto the grassy ground. Before I could scramble to my bike, I tumbled down into the ditch and now the sixth graders were there. I had cuts and bruises and I didn't know what to do.

All of a sudden, though, Jake grabbed me and my bike and we were gone! I was kind of weak but I kept up with Jake. When we got home, I told my mom about what had happened that day and the day before. I got grounded for a week, but I was just happy I was home and safe. The sixth graders had to do community service for a whole month!

At school everyone is asking questions and blabbing about what happened, but I am back to the same old schedule, the same old everything, except we have a new family member... Buddy, our golden retriever.

Aiden Nagorski, Grade 4
Bailey Elementary School, Woodbury
Teaching Artist, Stephen Peters

My Mom's a Spy

If only I knew what would happen. It was a bright and early morning, and boy was I grumpy. I had stayed up all night working on my homework. When my mom woke me, I just moaned, even though I knew she was in a hurry.

About ten minutes later, I got up and went to eat breakfast. There, my brother was eating every last bit of my toast. I told my mom but all she said was, "He's only a child." Uuuggghhhh! I couldn't believe it! I was just so grumpy that I had a scowl on my face the whole day.

I got home from school, home alone, as usual…or, at least that is what I thought. For some reason, my mom was home. She said, "We are moving now! So get packed!"

Two weeks later, we were living out in the country, somewhere in Wyoming instead of our home in Texas. The only person who lives close by is grouchy Mr. Ferguson. I don't like anything about him! Here are some reasons why:
1. He has a cat named Charles (P.S. he doesn't have a dog named Sam, like me);
2. He didn't even help my mom when my brother got sick!
3. Once his cat got lost and he said, "It's your fault."
And lastly, 4. He doesn't believe anything!

Anyway, one day I was looking for special rocks and I got lost! And guess what. I was lost in Mr. Ferguson's corn field on harvest day! Just then, I heard a sound like "wrrrr, wrrrr, wrrrr!"

Oh, no! It was Mr. Ferguson's combine! I ran as fast as I could in the opposite direction as the sounds. I got out of the corn field and arrived home safely.

"Boy," I thought to myself. "That was an adventure!"

One day, after lunch, my mom told me why we moved. She said she was a secret agent. And she was sent here to Wyoming to investigate…Mr. Ferguson!
(To be continued…)

Charlotte Mitlyng, Grade 4
Hilltop Primary School, Minnetrista
Teaching Artist, Kelly Barnhill

The Most Amazing Letter!

One day Lucy got off the school bus at her house in the country. She wondered if she got some mail. She loved getting mail! It was one of her favorite things she ever got. When she looked in the mailbox, there was only one letter. Lucy took out the letter and read who the letter was for. Surprisingly, it was for her!

She quickly opened it. It was from her older sister, Sarah. It said, "I was wondering if you could come help me here in Arizona because I'm going on a trip to Hollywood for my job. I wonder if you and Mom could come and watch over my house while I am gone. Tell me if you can come. Love, Sarah."

Lucy ran up the steps of her house and almost tripped on her shoelaces. She ran in yelling, "Mom! Mom, look what I got in the mail! It's from Sarah!"

"Whoa, honey! Let me see," said Mom. Her mom read it over and said, "We're definitely going. Let's wait for your father to come home with your baby brother Harold."

When her father came home, Lucy started yelling, "Dad! Dad, look what I got in the mail!"

When Dad read the letter he thought it was the most amazing letter he had ever seen. At bedtime, Lucy asked her mom if she could take the letter to school tomorrow to show her class. "Sure, honey," said her mom, "but remember not to lose it. Okay?" Lucy promised.

The next day in school she showed it to her friend Mouse and told her the story. "She even has a cat as fat as a barrel," said Lucy. Then, as she told the rest of the story, the biggest bully in school, Jasper, came and snatched the letter out of her hands without even asking to look at it! Once he read it, he said, "This is the weirdest letter ever!" Jasper roared with laughter. Lucy ran all the way to her classroom and told on Jasper. Of course he got in trouble, but he still wouldn't give the letter back.

Lucy told her mom what happened when she got home. Her mom said, "Well, I have a surprise for you. Do you know what it is? I'll tell you. Tomorrow you are going to Arizona!"

Lucy was so excited she forgot about what had happened. "Mom," she asked, "could Mouse come with me?"

"Sure," said Mom. "It wouldn't hurt to have her come along."

Just then the phone rang. It was Jasper's mom. She said that Jasper had Lucy's letter and would drop it off at her house in a little bit.

"That's great," said Lucy's mom. "Now, honey, you have to go upstairs and pack your bags."

Lucy didn't want to pack her bags but she had to. When she opened her suitcase, she found a little kitten in there! She had been wishing for a cat for ages! Lucy ran all the way down the steps and into the kitchen yelling, "Mom, look! I found a kitten in my suitcase!"

"Good for you, honey!"

Then Lucy knew who put the kitten in her suitcase… it was Mom! Lucy went back upstairs with her kitten in her hands, cuddling her. When she was back upstairs she found no more surprises and finished packing her bags, ate supper, and went to bed early so she wouldn't be crabby in the morning.

Lauren Stueber, Grade 3
Park Elementary School, Le Sueur
Teaching Artist, Stephen Peters

Emily and the Portal to Ralana

Emily sat on her porch glaring around. Who would want to live here? It was horrible in every way but if she had to live here, she might as well go check it out. She got up and opened the door. "Mom, I am going to go check out the new neighborhood!" She didn't even wait for an answer, just slammed the door shut. Bam! Emily began walking through the neighborhood (if you could even call it that). But that's when she noticed the shimmering air.

Emily had been trying to figure out all day why the air was shimmering like that, it just wasn't natural. The most reasonable suggestion that Emily could think of was to walk right through so that's exactly what she did.

Suddenly, Emily sat up. Where was she? It looked like she was in a dense forest but, strangely, there wasn't any noise. Not a single bird singing, not a single cricket chirping. There was nothing, anything to give her even a hint to tell her where she was. She found no roads, not even a sign. All she saw were green fields of grass, a few dandelions and more trees. Where was everybody? But that's when she heard the low moans of an animal. Emily decided to follow the sound, especially when it seemed to be the only one. She set off to an unknown adventure.

When she finally arrived closer to the creature's low earthly moans she decided to take a rest. She sat on a rock beside the low moans. It was as quiet as the middle of the night. After a short rest, she got up again and headed off. Towards the sound.

When she finally pushed away the last vine she came upon a lion laying on the ground. "Hello," she said uncertainly.

"Oh, hello," the lion said. Emily jumped back. "You can talk!" she said. "Of course I can talk," said the lion. "What did you think?" he growled. "Now, are you going to help me get this thorn out of my paw or not?" he asked. Emily stared at him for a minute.

Then she shook her head as if to try and understand the fact that he could talk. "Yes, I will help you," Emily finally said. As Emily got closer to the lion she realized how majestic the lion really was: his mane flowing around him like the sun, his blue eyes seeming to look right through her. Emily knelt down and quickly ripped the thorn out of the lion's paw. The lion screamed. "Yeeow!!!"

"Are you all right?" she asked. The lion dipped his paw in a nearby pond, he didn't respond. "Where did you get that thorn from anyway?" Emily asked.

"The witch," the lion said.

Soon afterward, Emily had left the lion. He had asked her to go defeat the witch once and for all, but Emily had replied quite furiously, "I don't know anything about this place!" The lion had replied quite unhelpfully, saying she would figure it out and would not say anymore. So Emily had left and started walking, although she had no idea where to go. She had been walking for a while when suddenly she heard a rustling sound in the bushes. She bent down to look closer at the rustling creature, when it jumped out and pinned her to the ground, then left just like that. When she tried to get up she realized that she was stuck to the ground with some gooey substance.

After a full hour on the ground, Emily heard a jingling of bells in the distance. The sound was getting closer. She tried to look up (the best that she could) and saw a sleigh up in the sky pulled by two brilliant white winged horses. When they started to descend, she finally got a glimpse of the rider: a beautiful woman in a long, white dress and a sparkling crown on her black hair. "Who are you?" Emily asked.

"I am Zarina, but most people know me as 'the witch.'"

That's when Emily knew she had to get out of there before the witch decided to capture her and take her prisoner. She started to squirm there on the ground where she lay. "No need for that!" the witch said, and with a wave of her hand the gooey substance disappeared like it had never been there. Emily got up slowly. "Now just wait there while I grab something," said the witch casually. A little too casually, Emily thought. She wasn't going to wait and find out what the witch had in store for her—she turned around and ran.

After running for several minutes, Emily jumped behind a bush to rest. She lay behind the bush, thinking. She now knew how powerful the witch was, and she knew she couldn't defeat her without help. She got up and began running again, running towards a new adventure. An adventure where—she hoped—she would find friends to help her understand this new world, friends that would help her defeat the witch.

Charlotte Carlston, Grade 4
Bailey Elementary School, Woodbury
Teaching Artist, Stephen Peters

The Flood

The movie made me shiver. I yelped and threw the popcorn over my shoulder. It collided with the mop, which fell and knocked the food cart forward and a rope on the cart snagged my foot. With me snagged on the rope, which was tied to the cart, I was going at top speed down the dark aisle of the movie theatre. I screamed!

"Alleeexxxxx!" My friend Max screamed as the food cart hit the movie screen and rebounded, hitting the janitor's cart. Mops, cleaners, and cleaning supplies fell everywhere. The food cart, the janitor's cart locked into it, and me screaming hurtled out past the exit door. I hurtled onto the street and Max ran after me. Finally, the cart stopped and Max untied me.

"I'm so stupid," I moaned.

"You'll get over it," said Max.

"But what will my parents and the movie theatre guys say?" I moaned.

Just then it started to rain. "Run into the theatre!" yelled Max. "Our houses are too far away!"

As we ran in we heard an announcement on the loud speaker. "People at the theatre, there will be a flash flood. I'll be contacting your parents. We'll stay here for the night. Have a good time and don't panic."

"He tells us!?" I said.

"We might as well make the best of it," exclaimed Max.

"Look," I exclaimed excitedly. "There's an arcade. Want to play me?"

"Yeah!!"

We played for a while before water leaked through the speakers. "Climb to a higher place!" I yelled as water leaked in through the doors.

We ran up the stairs back into the main lobby, which was filling up with water. People ran left and right. We followed a group of kids back into the theatre mad up the stairs where the movie was still playing. The water was up to our knees now. An announcement came over the speakers, saying, "Everybody proceed to the roof!"

So we climbed up the emergency exit where there was a crowd of people. Suddenly and violently, Max and I got knocked off the roof with some other kids onto an upside down floating car. As we floated away, I got an idea.

"How about we pull off the bars on the bottom of the car and use them as paddles?" I said.

"But we can't pull them off," said another kid.

"Then we can grab a branch from that passing tree and use it to cling onto that house we are going to pass," Max said, pointing to a tree, then to a house way past the tree. When we got to the tree, I grabbed the branch with both hands while Max held the car in place. My hands and feet were slipping. I directed my weight backwards towards the car. The branch cracked and I tried to spin around, but my feet slipped and I fell into the churning water. Max grabbed the branch as my throat filled with water. Then Max pulled the branch and I was aboard again.

Max and I aimed the branch onto the latch of the door on the house so we could all climb onto the roof of the house just as the car sank and the branch snapped.

About an hour later, a plane came and carried us to my house. My parents were so happy to see us.

Atticus Wolford, Grade 5
Meadowbrook Elementary School, Golden Valley
Teaching Artist, Stephen Peters

Forgotten Kingdom

Old Kingdom of Adraylia
The long forgotten past
The halls whisper stories to you about the battles
Listen closely, hear the pictures

This history so old and forgotten
Memories tangled like grandmother's yarn
You try to see, you try to remember
But it's like wearing someone else's shoes
Looking in the mirror, but it's all a ruse

The Gathering Hall once full of celebrations
An adventure waiting to be started
Like a new book, yet to be opened
You want to explore
You are a caged bird, without a door
The kingdom looked like a sunrise
Extravagant, it's there to mesmerize

You pass by the kitchen
The redolent smell drives up your nose
Here, where once beautiful aromas roamed the halls
Like the fresh smells of the bakery
Reminding you of Mother's old recipes
Ahh, the Saturday nights, so savory
The smells so strong, like medicine, a necessity

Memories jump at you like muggers in the darkness
The memories are once again reunited
With a helpless roaming soul
Like the desert reunited with rain
Like an addict reunited with cocaine
Like a kiss reunited with lips
Like actors reunited with scripts

You pass the dungeons, Drip, Drip, Drip
Spider webs, skulls everywhere, an abandoned ship

Time passed another gift to see
Yet these walls speak a different story
Devoid of joy from the time of their birth
They hold prisoners, what are their souls worth
To live out a life of pain and suffering
Like a caged mind, with no wondering
These walls speak a story
For all to hear
Only a few can live out their glory
While the others are destined to disappear

You come out to the courtyard
Flowers lay scattered
Like drops of paint on a painter's easel
Resting quietly, patiently among others
To gently decorate the canvas

Death wears a disguise
A shot across the bow
An apple in my eyes
It's clear, now crystal
Skeletons in uniforms
Swords clattered on the ground
You want to leave at the drop of a hat
But you chew yourself out and keep it at that

You hear a loud scream
You look to the side and drop
You look around with a strangled expression

You lay on the ground
You realize that some stayed
In the place that won't be found...

Aditya Rewalliwar, Grade 8
South View Middle School, Edina
Teaching Artist, Frank Sentwali

All Because of a Storm

BOOM! The thunder crackled.

There was a girl in the city named Brittany who had an embarrassing fear of storms. She had only told her best friends –Emma, Alexis, and Maneejae—about this. She was in her last year of high school and she worried that if her secret got out she wouldn't get into a good college. Luckily, when this storm came, she had her friends at her house. They were perfect together. They were doing homework when they heard it again. BOOM! "Eeek!" Brittany screamed.

"It's okay," Maneejae said to calm her.

"You know, you should get over this fear," Alexis said.

"ALEXIS!" Emma screamed.

One second later Alexis was gone. All they saw was a shadow reaching over. Emma wanted to call 911, but Brittany's phone wasn't working. The friends spent the night at Brittany's house even though her apartment was very small.

"So, what do you think happened to her?" Brittany asked everyone.

"I don't know," said Maneejae, "but if we get to sleep we'll have more answers in the morning."

BOOM! CRACKLE!

"This is why I don't like storms," said Brittany.

"Yea. They're as scary as a duckling" said Emma rudely.

"Emma! That's so rude!" screeched Maneejae.

"Sorry," said Emma with attitude.

"Guys. Let's try to go to sleep," said Brittany, trying to end the conversation.

It was a long night. To be precise, it seemed to be longer than any night. Finally, morning came and the girls were ready to investigate. Emma found a piece of small, wrinkled paper on the ground. It said it was a free flight for three people to Italy. The girls were sure that if they went to Italy they would find more clues.

But just when they thought their plan was foolproof, they forgot one thing: The Mom. Brittany's mom, to be exact. Her mom was Claire and she was very worried about the girls' safety. It takes forever to get her mom to understand, and then it still doesn't work.

Once night fell and all Brittany's friends went home, she and her mom had a long talk. It was now time for Brittany to come clean and tell her mom about Alexis. "Why didn't you tell me about this before?" Claire asked.

Brittany shrugged for an answer. They compromised for Claire to come with them to Italy. Brittany was as excited as a kid about to have her braces taken off. She could barely sleep that night.

Finally, the day came. They met at the airport, where Claire paid for her ticket. The boring flight took forever, but finally—after two days with disgusting airplane food—they arrived in the gorgeous country of Italy. There was so much to see! So much to explore!

The friends found the sweatshirt Alexis was wearing the last time they saw her. They followed the clues to a big ugly shack. When they went in the door they heard a loud bang!

"ALEXIS!" they screamed together.

"Mmmmmmh!" Alexis tried to yell. She had blue duct tape on her mouth and on her arms and legs. There was a yellowish note taped to the chair she sat in.

The note, you ask? I'm saving that for the next story. BOOK TWO coming to your local stores soon!

Sophia Davig, Grade 4
Hilltop Elementary School, Henderson
Teaching Artist, Stephen Peters

William's Cash

William was riding the bus home. It was of course raining. He was getting off the bus when two gangsters walked into him. "Hey, what you doing, kid?" said the short one.

"Nothing," said William.

"Hey, kid, where you going?" said the tall one.

"Home," William mumbled.

"Why don't you go through that alley?" the short one said.

"I can't go there," said William.

"Oh, it will be much easier," said the tall one. "Your mommy will be glad."

William wondered if it would be the right choice. Suddenly the tall one took off his gray cap. In it was $300. William's eyes widened. He took the cap and ran.

"Ha! Ha!" the tall one laughed. "That's the money we took from the bank!"

BEE—DO! BBE-DO! A police car stopped William in his tracks.

"It was him!" yelled the short gangster. The two gangsters were dressed as citizens. "He stole the money," said the tall one.

The officer put William in the car with handcuffs. The officer confiscated the cash. "So," the officer said as they drove away, "stealing cash, ay?"

"No," said William.

"That's what everybody says," said the officer. They drove to the police department. The officer put William in a cell, then the chief officer walked in. "What's that kid doing?" said the chief.

"He was caught stealing $300," said the officer. "His mom was contacted."

The chief walked away. "I'm getting donuts, Jeff," he said.

William started smelling smoke. BOOM! The entrance door fell off its hinges and a robber ran in with keys. He unlocked every cell. The hair on the back of William's neck stood up. He fainted. When he woke up he was in the back of a car. Jeff was driving. "What did he look like?" asked Jeff.

"Who?" asked William.

"The robber," said Jeff.

"Oh, he had black hair and… wait a minute! That was a gangster! The gangster that tricked me," said William. Then the side door opened and William flew out into the river like a torpedo.

SPLOOSH! He was swimming toward the shore. "Arrgh!" yelled William, as a spotlight blinded him. A helicopter landed in front of him. It took him to Jeff's car. "Okay, kid?" Jeff asked. William got in the car. They were chasing someone.

Jeff explained how they caught the real bank robbers. Security cameras! Now they were chasing them. Okay, William thought, high speed chase. William explained how the gangsters had tricked him and freed their friends from jail.

Jeff's car was slipping on the icy roads as they caught sight of the gangsters' car. As Jeff passed the gangsters, he opened the sun roof. "Here," Jeff said, handing William a saw. "Stop them!"

William jumped through the sun roof onto the other car. He started sawing a hole in the top of the car. Jeff's car drove forward. CLANG! The hole opened on the car. William jumped in. "Hey!" yelled the tall gangster. The short one turned around and was just about to punch William. "Boss! The ice!"

Too late. SLIP! CRASH! They crashed into the side of the bridge.

BEE-DO! BEE-DO!

It was Jeff. William sighed a sigh of relief. Jeff arrested the gangsters and took William home. He'd had a crazy day, so he ran to his mom and then went to bed.

Wyatt Cummings, Grade 4
Roseau Elementary School, Roseau
Teaching Artist, Stephen Peters

Section 7:
Wondering

In My Head

In my head is a hawk flying free
A shadow creeping up the wall
The stars in the sky
Where my last name came from
What my life as an adult will be like
Where all the English words come from
What it would be like if I was blind
And if I didn't have friends
And if I never went to school
What life would be like
If I didn't do things.

Natalie Hughes, Grade 2
Gleason Lake Elementary School, Plymouth
Teaching Artist, Julia Klatt Singer

Stars

Ever think of yourself as being a single star in the night sky?
I mean if you look at it you are one out of 7.5 billion people on this earth.
How are you supposed to make a difference?
You are just one single person.
Well, look at it this way you could be that star that just so happens to light up our entire world.
Our sun is just one big star.
We rely on this star to maintain our planet in a matter where we are able to live.
You could be the star or spark inside of somebody's eyes with whom you love; they are in love with you.
A single star will always have the chance to affect something or somebody bigger.
Like the universe before the earth.
There was just nothingness until eventually, from a star, there was enough energy to create this incredible planet.
On which we all live.
We are all special, we all make a difference in the ways that really matter.
You are the best thing you could ever be.
You are you.
Do not count yourself out.
You are the most incredible person in this world.
You have a destiny and you have to be the one to fulfill it.
No one can achieve your goals for you.
Just do it.
Don't let your memes be dreams.

Faith Rudnick, Grade 12
Brainerd Learning Center, Brainerd
Teaching Artist, Saymoukda Vongsay

Mansion

My mind has been called many things
The best being a mansion
Where I have a home for my thoughts
But I'm in desperate need for an expansion
I just cannot work with the space I got
I need somewhere where my thoughts can roam
Inside these guarded walls
A place where my mind has a home
Where it can run down the halls
I let my mind grow
With inspiring ideas
And when I let my mind go
I can find peace within us
And then I will finally know
Who I am inside my head
Because then I can show
The person locked away in their bed
To the outside world surrounding us
Where almost no one truly knows who I am
Not the people on the city bus
Or even the teacher I call "ma'am"
None of them know the poor girl hidden
Under modest clothes and an old class ring
So now I sit here with this delicate black pen
And desperately try to ignore the sting
The sting
The sting
The sting of shame, and the sting of abuse
The collection of nightmares that come soon after ten
But I know now that it is no use
Because under your scrutinizing eyes, I sit like a hen

Nervous enough to take orders from you
But I'm done letting you just take over my mind then
So get out of my priceless mansion
You're not welcome inside
If my mind is a school, you're on suspension
And give me a chance to hide
My secrets are my very savior
The only one that knows who I am
Under all this classic good behavior
Is Silence of the Lambs
But despite all these useless references
I know that you're confused
What's behind the fence of my mansion, the electric fence?
That's what you get to choose
In all truth, I can be whatever you need
My mind is versatile
Like the warning I heed
Beware of your thoughts, they are vile
I should know better than anyone
That the game of insanity has already been won

Emma Joswiak-McLaughlin, Grade 9
Roosevelt High School, Minneapolis
Teaching Artist, Frank Sentwali

I Prefer

I prefer myself over you
I prefer good times over bad
Yes over no
I don't hang with people who prefer fake
Over friendship
I prefer today over yesterday
Most of the time, I prefer loud over quiet
I prefer pop over soda
Food over exercise
I prefer time over change
Carpets over rugs
Sleep over bedtime
Friends over bullies
Fun over homework
Outside over inside

Miya Horel, Grade 7
FAIR School Crystal, Crystal
Teaching Artist, Alexei Moon Casselle

Dear God

Can you see me?
Can you see me talking to you, pouring my heart out to you?
But God, did you know I'm doubting you?
But you should know that right because you're the God that I was raised to know that you can see everything, hear everything, and know everything.
But God can you tell me why my mom died, she always prayed and never lied?
Please God listen to me.
I'm having a hard time believing you because I can't see you but still somehow I pray to you.
I grew up reading the bible but is the bible really you or is it just mankind creating you?
Do you have a plan for me?
Do you really know what I'm going to be?
Or is it just another game mankind created to make us think after we leave this world to keep hope in our eyes, to make us by being good, we will make it to an afterlife?
But there's all these wonders like how are you watching my every move but more than a thousand babies are born each day?
How do you choose who dies and who lives?
And why does life cause so much pain?
I know pain makes us strong but how do you pick and choose who to honor?
And how do you choose who to drop a miracle on?
People are just numbers, drawn at random?
Miracles are some f— lottery?
People say you're fake but how do you choose who to take?
Please God don't be mad that I have doubts about you.
But I have one last question, are you proud of me?

Santos Aguirre, Grade 7
Community of Peace Academy, Saint Paul
Teaching Artist, Frank Sentwali

Pearls of Wisdom

Creativity doesn't die it still goes on. – Ayamei Her

Creativity cannot be forced upon you, it must be let in.
– Jacob King

Creativity is like medicine, you can't live without it.
– Isse Ahmed

Creativity is a disease that's very contagious and everyone has it. – Ashwaq Aliyow

Creativity comes from your mind and imagination.
– Alexander Bagdade

Before you create you have to eat because it's in the word.
– Raniya Abawari

Creativity comes from the world of imagination.
– Eyoel Enkuebahry

Creativity is like matter, it makes up everything in the universe. – Louis Sloot

Creativity is life. – Ari Goldberg

Mrs. Goetzke's Class, Grade 5
Capitol Hill Gifted and Talented Magnet, Saint Paul
Teaching Artist, T. Mychael Rambo

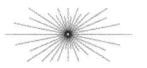

Common Sense

Knowledge is power, and ignorance is bliss
In a world that's slowly disappearing
Suffocating, can't breathe with all these toxins
Toxins like racism, poverty and so much more
Waiting patiently for the door to open
To those who are not quick to notice the hopeless
'Cause they can't recognize the signs and the omens
That are leading to the final conclusion of
Magic and potions are the only solutions

Ignorance is bliss
In a world that's slowly disappearing
Knowledge is power
In a world that is capable of change and success
And knowledge has led man to the path of progress
And for this we send salutations to Common Sense

In this new year we mourn the death of an old friend
Who once said that ignorance was not bliss
He was the rescuer when we fell into the depths of an abyss
We need him back to surround us with composure
Before the world turns to the ultimate closure

He left with no warning, no reason
Or time to make a last wish
Our obituary is Common Sense
Who lived in cold, hard silence
Now all we have in this world is the screeching sound of sirens

The world can't run without his threshold
He left us in vain without any ending quote
He left us without any head to the throne
Without your guidance we are lost
Yet have nothing to lose
In his life, he taught us a few tunes
Rest in peace Common Sense, our true friend

Eman Abdullahi, Sundus Mohamed and Suado Muqtasid,
Grade 10
Rochester STEM Academy, Rochester
Teaching Artist, Frank Sentwali

Untitled Assumptions

Assumptions advocate blasphemy of social corruptness
Words speak louder than they theorize
The concept of unethicality they sterilize
The perspective of subordinate attribute, they sterilize
Remorseless as they accumulate off the cries
Equality they represent but act upon us as picayune
Conduct designated to thwart sin
But the bottomless pit they draw you in
Exacerbate but when confronted
Act as if it is impossible to commemorate

D. N., Grade 8
North View Middle School, Brooklyn Park
Teaching Artist, Tou SaiKo Lee

Confusion Is an Ocean

Stranded boats
In a vast blue

Waves crashing on each other
Not knowing what direction to go

Everything looks the same
For miles on end

Nowhere to go now
Except down

Until a small strip of land appears
And everything becomes clear.

Ella Helgeson, Grade 10
Roseau Secondary School, Roseau
Teaching Artist, Julia Klatt Singer

Highway Corner

Driving by
The highway corner
Light was red, we lurch to a stop.
Always a woman at the corner
With a cardboard sign.
"Please help no money soon going to have a baby."
I feel bad for her,
Sad for her.
Tears started trickling down
The back of my eyes.

The next week's drive
By the highway corner
Light is red, we lurch to a stop.
She's not there. But an old man is.
What happened to her?
Did she pass away?
When she was giving birth?
Or is she struggling, all alone?
Where did she go?
The light turns green.
We go.
I never see her again
When we drive by
The highway corner
When the light is red.

Kate Hanf, Grade 5
Saint Paul Academy Lower School, Saint Paul
Teaching Artist, Julia Klatt Singer

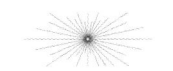

The Playground (from different ages)

I look out over the mountainous expanse
of playground equipment
a kingdom
for me to run
climbing the royal steps
run across the bridge
glide down the slide
back again
the greatest fun.

Feeling like a ninja
the playground
my obstacle course.
Who can run it fastest?
I can!
Running up the slide
swinging from the monkey bars
training to be the next
American Ninja Warrior.

I'd rather not be here.
I'm too old
Playgrounds are for kids
but . . . I suppose if we're here.
Tag! You're it.
Racing through the equipment
getting that first time thrill
the adrenaline of the park.

Watching my siblings
play, laugh, run
worth it
to come
to the playground
even though
I've outgrown
the slides and bars.
I swing.
I watch.
I smile.

It's not what I remember.
Rusted colors chipping
from dull metal.
Too tall to swing
from the bars
scooting down the slide
less of a glide
too big.
I've grown
away
from the playground.

Eavan Bobbe, Grade 6
Oak View Middle School, Anoka
Teaching Artist, Susan Marie Swanson

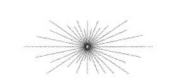

2016-17 Index by Student Writer

Abdi	Ayub	Rochester STEM Academy	9
Abdullahi	Eman	Rochester STEM Academy	149
Abdullahi	Ekhlas	Rochester STEM Academy	41
Aguirre	Santos	Community of Peace Academy	147
Alkhatib	Juman	Creek Valley Elementary	14
Ammann	Jack Dennis	Le Sueur-Henderson Middle	23
Awad	Nasrin	Rochester STEM Academy	37
Bagley	Sarah	Creek Valley Elementary	68
Becker	Shea	Meadowbrook Elementary	50
Bobbe	Eavan	Oak View Middle School	154
Breen	Brody	Oak Ridge Elementary	53
Carlston	Charlotte	Bailey Elementary School	128
C.	S.	Roosevelt Senior High School	97
Cotter	Adrian	Mendota Elementary School	52
Crone	Amelia	Anwatin Middle School	3
Crosby's Class	Mr.	St. Anthony Park Elementary	51
Cummings	Wyatt	Roseau Elementary School	137
Dahl	Hailey	Roseau Secondary School	13
Daniels	Annelise	Oak Hill Montessori School	106
Davig	Sophia	Hilltop Elementary School	135
Del Carmen	Beatrix	Perpich Center for Arts Education	44
Dosch	Lucy	Capitol Hill Gifted & Talented	75
E.	N. A.	Brainerd Learning Center	114
Eh Say	Htoo	Humboldt Secondary School	95
Ekman	Elizabeth	Meadowbrook Elementary	118
Eldredge	Frannie	Mendota Elementary	55
Elftmann	Signe	Hillcrest Community School	69
Fernandez	Samantha	Oak View Middle School	62
Furness Rubio	Cristina	Richfield Middle School	24
Gao Ia Yang	Kathy	Humboldt Secondary School	108
Goetzke's Class	Mrs.	Capitol Hill Gifted & Talented	148
Hagg	Hannah	Gleason Lake Elementary	56
Hanf	Kate	St. Paul Academy - Lower School	153
Helgeson	Ella	Roseau Secondary School	152
Her	Michaelsan	Community of Peace Academy	93
Hilton	Henry	St. Paul Academy - Lower School	28
Horel	Miya	FAIR School Crystal	146
Hughes	Natalie	Gleason Lake Elementary	142
Hydrie	Karina	Capitol Hill Gifted & Talented	74
Ibrahim	Mahamed	Rochester STEM Academy	35

Jama	Bushra	Rochester STEM Academy	11
Johnstun	Daisy	Roseau Secondary School	98
Joswiak-McLaughlin	Emma	Roosevelt Senior High	144
Lay	Lay	Humboldt Secondary School	6
Johnson	Natalia L.	Roseau Secondary School	22
Lucía Luna Apodaca	Sara	Richfield Middle School	16
Lueck	Dakota	Hillcrest Community School	2
M.	M.	Roosevelt Senior High School	33
Markfort	Noah	Bailey Elementary School	39
Mitlyng	Charlotte	Hilltop Primary School	124
Mohamed	Dahabo	Richfield Middle School	29
Mohamed	Sundus	Rochester STEM Academy	149
Mohamed	Nafiso	Rochester STEM Academy	41
Muqtasid	Suado	Rochester STEM Academy	149
Myers	Hannah	South View Middle School	90
Nagorski	Aiden	Bailey Elementary School	122
Napierala's Class	Mrs.	Highland Park Elementary	8
N.	D.	North View IB World School	151
Opitz	Max	South View Middle School	63
P. G.	V.	North View IB World School	77
P.	L.	North View IB World School	71
Puklich	Tavie	Hilltop Primary School	58
Raya	Ivy	St. Paul Academy - Upper School	15
Reichgelt's Class	Mrs.	La Crescent-Hokah Middle	80
Rewalliwar	Aditya	South View Middle School	133
Reynolds	Gianna	Mendota Elementary	57
Rosenquist	Allison	Oak Hill Montessori	46
Rudnick	Faith	Brainerd Learning Center	143
Schoening	Skyllar	Roseau Secondary School	111
Solomon	Matia	North View IB World School	34
Steinborn	Rylee	Le Sueur-Henderson Middle	5
Stovall	Qais	Lake Harriet Upper School	59
Stueber	Lauren	Park Elementary School	126
Sumera	Megan	Roosevelt Senior High School	38
Tafelmeyer	Kensington	Kittson Central Elementary	21
Terrones' Class	Mr.	St. Anthony Park Elementary	65
Torrence	Susana	Royal Oaks Elementary	61
Tuck	Elliott	White Bear Lake Central Middle	105
Vasquez	Gabrianna	Edison Senior High School	76
Vergara	Mauricio Q.	Richfield Middle School	31

Warsame	Abdirahman	Rochester STEM Academy	19
Wolff	Maverick	St. Paul Academy - Upper School	54
Wolford	Atticus	Meadowbrook Elementary	131
Yang	Muajtsim (TJ)	North View IB World School	78
Yusuf	Mustafa	Rochester STEM Academy	35

2016-17 Index by School

Anwatin Middle School	Amelia	Crone	3
Bailey Elementary School	Charlotte	Carlston	128
Bailey Elementary School	Noah	Markfort	39
Bailey Elementary School	Aiden	Nagorski	122
Brainerd Learning Center	N. A.	E.	114
Brainerd Learning Center	Faith	Rudnick	143
Capitol Hill Gifted & Talented	Lucy	Dosch	75
Capitol Hill Gifted & Talented	Mrs. Goetzke's	Class	148
Capitol Hill Gifted & Talented	Karina	Hydrie	74
Community of Peace Academy	Santos	Aguirre	147
Community of Peace Academy	Michaelsan	Her	93
Creek Valley Elementary	Juman	Alkhatib	14
Creek Valley Elementary	Sarah	Bagley	68
Edison Senior High School	Gabrianna	Vasquez	76
FAIR School Crystal	Miya	Horel	146
Gleason Lake Elementary	Hannah	Hagg	56
Gleason Lake Elementary	Natalie	Hughes	142
Highland Park Elementary	Mrs. Napierala's	Class	8
Hillcrest Community School	Signe	Elftmann	69
Hillcrest Community School	Dakota	Lueck	2
Hilltop Elementary School	Sophia	Davig	135
Hilltop Primary School	Charlotte	Mitlyng	124
Hilltop Primary School	Tavie	Puklich	58
Humboldt Secondary School	Htoo	Eh Say	95
Humboldt Secondary School	Kathy	Gao Ia Yang	108
Humboldt Secondary School	Lay	Lay	6
Kittson Central Elementary	Kensington	Tafelmeyer	21
La Crescent-Hokah Middle	Mrs. Reichgelt's	Class	80
Lake Harriet Upper School	Qais	Stovall	59
Le Sueur-Henderson Middle	Jack Dennis	Ammann	23
Le Sueur-Henderson Middle	Rylee	Steinborn	5
Meadowbrook Elementary	Shea	Becker	50
Meadowbrook Elementary	Elizabeth	Ekman	118
Meadowbrook Elementary	Atticus	Wolford	131
Mendota Elementary	Adrian	Cotter	52
Mendota Elementary	Frannie	Eldredge	55
Mendota Elementary	Gianna	Reynolds	57
North View IB World School	D.	N.	151
North View IB World School	V.	P.G.	77
North View IB World School	L.	P.	71

North View IB World School	Matia	Solomon	34
North View IB World School	Muajtsim (TJ)	Yang	78
Oak Hill Montessori	Annelise	Daniels	106
Oak Hill Montessori	Allison	Rosenquist	46
Oak Ridge Elementary	Brody	Breen	53
Oak View Middle School	Eavan	Bobbe	154
Oak View Middle School	Samantha	Fernandez	62
Park Elementary School	Lauren	Stueber	126
Perpich Center for Arts Education	Beatrix	Del Carmen	44
Richfield Middle School	Cristina	Furness Rubio	24
Richfield Middle School	Sara	Lucía Luna Apodaca	16
Richfield Middle School	Dahabo	Mohamed	29
Richfield Middle School	Mauricio	Vergara Quiroz	31
Rochester STEM Academy	Ayub	Abdi	9
Rochester STEM Academy	Eman	Abdullahi	149
Rochester STEM Academy	Ekhlas	Abdullahi	41
Rochester STEM Academy	Nasrin	Awad	37
Rochester STEM Academy	Mahamed	Ibrahim	35
Rochester STEM Academy	Bushra	Jama	11
Rochester STEM Academy	Sundus	Mohamed	149
Rochester STEM Academy	Nafiso	Mohamed	41
Rochester STEM Academy	Suado	Muqtasid	149
Rochester STEM Academy	Abdirahman	Warsame	19
Rochester STEM Academy	Mustafa	Yusuf	35
Roosevelt Senior High	S.	C.	97
Roosevelt Senior High	Emma	Joswiak-McLaughlin	144
Roosevelt Senior High	M.	M.	33
Roosevelt Senior High	Megan	Sumera	38
Roseau Elementary School	Wyatt	Cummings	137
Roseau Secondary School	Hailey	Dahl	13
Roseau Secondary School	Ella	Helgeson	152
Roseau Secondary School	Daisy	Johnstun	98
Roseau Secondary School	Natalia L.	Johnson	22
Roseau Secondary School	Skyllar	Schoening	111
Royal Oaks Elementary	Susana	Torrence	61
St. Anthony Park Elementary	Mr. Crosby's	Class	51
St. Anthony Park Elementary	Mr. Terrones'	Class	65
St. Paul Academy - Lower School	Kate	Hanf	153
St. Paul Academy - Lower School	Henry	Hilton	28
St. Paul Academy - Upper School	Ivy	Raya	15
St. Paul Academy - Upper School	Maverick	Wolff	54

South View Middle School	Hannah	Myers	90
South View Middle School	Max	Opitz	63
South View Middle School	Aditya	Rewalliwar	133
White Bear Lake Central Middle	Elliott	Tuck	105

2016-17 COMPAS Creative Classroom Teaching Writers

- Fiona Avocado
- Kelly Barnhill
- Becca Barniskis
- Alexei Moon Casselle
- Desdamona
- Taous Khazem
- Tou SaiKo Lee
- May Lee-Yang
- Charlie Maguire
- Rachel Moritz
- Kyle "Guante" Tran Myhre
- Adam Gabriel Napoli-Rangel
  (aka SEE MORE PERSPECTIVE)
- Marie Olofsdotter
- Stephen Peters
- T. Mychael Rambo
- Marcie Rendon
- Frank Sentwali
- Julia Klatt Singer
- Susan Marie Swanson
- Saymoukda Vongsay
- Levi Weinhagen

COMPAS works with over 100 of the top Teaching Artists in Minnesota. Our Roster of Artists includes writers, theater artists, visual artists, dancers, musicians, and more. To read more about these artists visit COMPAS.org.

COMPAS Mission and Programs

COMPAS uses the arts to unleash the creativity within all of us so we can create better lives and better communities.

Creative Classroom
Creativity is not owned by the arts, it is taught by them.

We connect students from kindergarten to 12th grade with the life-changing power of creativity, reaching over 30,000 school children across Minnesota each year. Our skilled teaching artists teach professional art techniques, build connections with classroom curriculum, explore history and cultural diversity, and nurture student creativity.

Creative Community
Those who create the art define the culture.

From libraries, parks and festivals to after school programs, youth employment programs, shelters and recreation centers, COMPAS delivers enriching, creativity-growing experiences to all Minnesotans.

Artful Aging™
Creativity gives us purpose. Purpose is what keeps us alive.

Artists work side-by-side with adults 55+ who live independently and in senior living centers. Engaging, artistic experiences bring joy and satisfaction to seniors as they discover new talents and renew old ones.

Arts in Healthcare
When words fail to express, creativity allows us to heal.

Our Arts in Healthcare programs strengthen community and wellness through professional arts performances and instruction. Creativity stimulates recovery, increases quality of life and connects staff and patients.

Our talented writers, musicians, visual artists and performers are ready to inspire all ages with hands-on programs throughout Minnesota.

For more information on any of these programs contact COMPAS at: 651.292.3249 or info@compas.org.

COMPAS Staff

- Betsy Mowry Voss, *Arts Innovation Director*
- Dawne Brown White, *Executive Director*
- Elwyn Ruud, *Northwest Area Arts Coordinator*
- Emma Seeley, *Arts Program & Marketing Coordinator*
- Huong Nguyen, *Finance & Administration Manager*
- Joan Linck, *Director of Strategic Development*
- Juliana Anderson Wilkins, *Director of External Relations*
- Julie Strand, *Arts Program Director*
- Lynne Beck, *Senior Grant Writer*
- Mica Lee Anders, *ArtsWork & Women's Writing Program Coordinator*
- Michael Salazar, *Arts & Marketing Assistant*

COMPAS Board of Directors

- Roderic Hernub Southall, *President*
- Mimi Stake (ex-officio), *Vice president*
- Susan Rotilie, *Vice president*
- Kathy Sanville, *Secretary*
- Jeff Goldenberg, *Treasurer*
- Cheryl Bock, *Executive Committee at-large*
- Samantha Massaglia, *Marketing & Communications*
- Yvette Trotman, *Executive Committee at-large*
- Keven Ambrus
- Mae Brooks
- Bob Erickson (ex-officio)
- Jessica Gessner
- Diane Johnson
- Christina Koppang
- Abby Lawrence
- Hristina Markova
- Celena Plesha
- Louis Porter II
- Mary Sennes
- Liz Sheets
- Michelle Silverman
- Virajita Singh
- Dameun Strange
- Walter L. Smith III

The Lillian Wright Awards for Creative Writing

The Lillian Wright Awards recognize literary achievement among young writers in the COMPAS Creative Classroom Program. Generously underwritten by the Lillian Wright and C. Emil Berglund Foundation, the award winners and their schools are celebrated at the publication event in December along with all the students within these pages. This year's judge is Daniel Gabriel.

The winners are:

- BEST WRITING, GRADES K-3:
  "*In My Head,*" by **Natalie Hughes**, Grade 2, Gleason Lake Elementary, Plymouth

- BEST PROSE, GRADES 4-6:
  "*One Beautiful Thing,*" by **Elizabeth Ekman,** Grade 5, Meadowbrook Elementary, Golden Valley

- BEST POETRY, GRADES 4-6:
  "*The Playground,*" by **Eavan Bobbe**, Grade 6, Oak View Middle School, Andover

- BEST WRITING, GRADE 7:
  "*Tongue Waltz,*" by **Cristina Furness Rubio**, Grade 7 Richfield Middle School, Richfield

- BEST WRITING, GRADE 8:
  "*The Roots Within Us,*" by **Lay Lay**, Grade 8, Humboldt High School, Saint Paul

- BEST POETRY, GRADES 9-12:
  "Of the Six Moro People Who Survived (a sestina),"
  by **Beatrix Del Carmen**, Grade 11,
  Perpich Center for Arts Education, Golden Valley

- BEST SPOKEN WORD, GRADES 9-12:
  "Anchor," by **Ekhlas Abdullahi & Nafiso Mohamed**,
  Grade 9, Rochester STEM Academy, Rochester

Lillian Wright Awards Judge

Daniel Gabriel is a former teaching artist and longtime Director of Arts Programming for COMPAS. His published work includes a novel (*Twice a False Messiah*) and two story collections (*Wrestling with Angels* and *Tales from the Tinker's Dam*), as well as hundreds of nonfiction articles on cultural immersion travel, baseball, rock 'n' roll, and the like. He was also the editor of previous COMPAS Anthologies of Student Writing, *Punch at the Wild Tornado* and *The River Starts Flowing*.

Thank you to our supporters, including:

The Lillian Wright and C. Emil Berglund Foundation

This activity is made possible by the voters of Minnesota through a grant from the Minnesota State Arts Board, thanks to a legislative appropriation from the arts and cultural heritage fund.

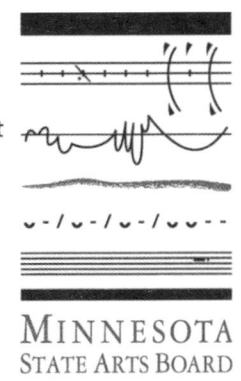

WE ARE ALL BORN *creative*
BUT WE MUST WORK TO STAY THAT WAY.

WHEN WE INVEST IN PRESERVING THIS PART OF OUR MINDS, WE HOLD ON TO A PIECE OF OURSELVES THAT MAKES US BETTER SUITED TO NOT ONLY SURVIVE IN THIS WORLD, BUT **THRIVE.**

OUR CREATIVITY *is precious*

WE CAN'T SQUANDER IT. WE CAN'T DEFUND IT. WE CAN'T LET IT BECOME EXTRACURRICULAR. BECAUSE IT'S NOT.

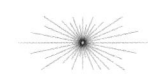

IT IS ESSENTIAL
it's ELEMENTAL
HEALING, TEACHING
LIFE-GIVING